Jim Marshall

Nancy Dubin

Judy Collins

by Vivian Claire

Flash Books
New York   London

Judy Collins

Copyright © Flash Books, 1977
All rights reserved.

International Standard Book Number:
0-8256-3914-X
Library of Congress Catalog Card Number:
77-78538
Printed in the United States of America

In Great Britain: Book Sales Ltd., 78 Newman
Street, London W1, England.
In Canada: Gage Trade Publishing, P.O. Box
5000, 164 Commander Blvd., Agincourt, Ontario
M1S 3C7.

Designed by Jon Goodchild
Discography by Wendy Schacter
Front cover photograph by Nancy Dubin
Back cover photograph by Jim Marshall

Contents

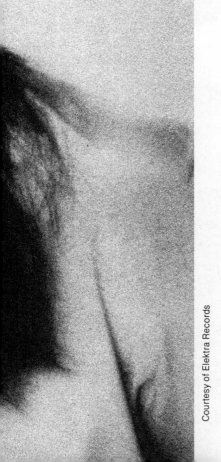

Courtesy of Elektra Records

Introduction

Jim Marshall

1.

The azure eyes stare out at you, serene and lovely. Her gaze suggests kindness, depth. Judy Collins may be a superstar, but as you look at her blue eyes from one album jacket to another, or if you are lucky enough to see her in concert, she does not have the distant, superior quality other superstars project. Judy Collins looks out at you like a friend.

In the early 1960s, when Judy Collins first began to make her extraordinary records, few people knew who she was. Today many of the other sixties singers have faded away, but Judy Collins' work has continued and grown. After fifteen albums, six of them gold, her fame now is so great that no one can really predict its limit. Her talent has exploded far beyond the confines of music. A brilliant songwriter and an amazingly talented vocal interpreter of others' songs, Collins has branched out into other fields, producing and co-directing a documentary movie nominated for an Academy Award, playing a role in a Central Park production of *Peer Gynt,* writing sensitively about her life in *The Judy Collins Songbook,* guest-hosting a television program, and being politically active in encouraging voter registration in Mississippi, supporting the defendants in the Chicago Seven trial, and currently working in the women's movement.

Judy Collins never made a comeback because she never went away. Her first albums of folk music caused *Time* magazine to hail her as a "major contender for the female folk crown." But even by the third album she was breaking out of the folk music mold. She doesn't care about labels. What matters to her about a song is not its "type" but simply whether she loves it. She has sung pieces from Broadway musicals and songs by the Rolling Stones.

Her richly expressive voice has a magical quality, her diction and phrasing, a crystalline clarity, and her sense of the dramatic is impeccable. The warm voice, enormous blue eyes, lovely, intense face framed by long, light-brown hair evoke a tremendous emotional response from audiences, making her a favorite in concert halls, on college campuses, and in homes throughout the country and the world. Teenagers and adults alike listen to her records. Her following has the intensity and commitment of a cult. Her fans are moved to tears or transfixed by beauty when she sings songs ranging from 14th-century French chansons to familiar American folk ballads, from Dylan's "Tommorrow is a Long Time" to Leonard Cohen's "Suzanne" to Sondheim's "Send in the Clowns."

But Judy Collins' story is not one of instant success. She didn't pick up a guitar one day and become famous the next. She worked long and hard to get where she is. She still works hard. There has been terrible pain in her life, but there has been joy, too. Today, at 38, her work is mature but still developing. The serenity in her eyes reveals a genuine artist, a woman who knows where she has been as well as where she's going.

Her Life

Jim Marshall

2.

Judy Collins was born May 1, 1939, in Seattle, and grew up in Denver, Colorado. Her father was blind but lived as though he could see. He insisted on self-sufficiency and refused to use a cane or a dog. Judy feels, looking back, that her mother denied herself a great deal, living for and through her handicapped husband and her five children.

Her father had been in show business for twenty years. He spent his childhood in a special school where children who were handicapped or deformed were lumped together to be ignored by society. But Charles Collins even then showed his mettle, his ambition. He formed a band at the special school in Idaho and worked his way through the University of Idaho playing. Later he did radio shows, the old-timey personal kind of radio shows that established a special rapport with the audience, for whom he mixed his music with a homespun optimistic philosophy.

Her father felt unfulfilled as a musician. Judy Collins was his first-born, and it was natural that he would want her to be a musician. She began to study piano at the age of five. No matter what the family's financial condition was, there was always money for her piano lessons.

In her lovely song "My Father," Judy pays tribute to Charles Collins in a series of lyrical images and gentle sounds:

My father always promised us that we
  would live in France.
We'd go boating on the Seine and I
  would learn to dance.
We lived in Ohio then and he worked
  in the mines.
Honest dreams, like boats, we knew,
  would sail in time.

When she was ten years old, Judy began to study classical piano with Dr. Antonia Brico in Denver. This was a great opportunity for the young musician. More than twenty years later Judy Collins was to make a documentary movie about her teacher called *Antonia: A Portrait of the Woman,* paying homage to this great person whose influence had been so important to her.

At ten Judy already knew that music was an indelible part of her life. She would be a musician, and that knowledge was ingrained in her. She did not question it. Her ambition, whether it came from herself, her father, or Dr. Brico, was already formed.

She loved Dr. Brico's house, which always smelled of grapefruit and rosin. She loved the studio around the corner in the same building, an enormous room with two grand Steinway pianos. On the walls of the studio were the photographs of students. There was a photo of Sibelius, with whom Dr. Brico had studied conducting when she was much younger. Its inscription read: "To Antonia with affectionate regards from Sibelius." Dr. Brico had conducted his orchestra in Finland on his 82nd birthday.

There were also many photographs of Dr. Albert Schweitzer, a close friend of Dr. Brico's, whom she visited every summer in Africa.

Judy Collins was totally in awe of her teacher, who wore long black skirts and conducted the Businessmen's Orchestra of Denver. Dr. Brico would cut Judy's nails when she came for her lessons. Judy has written about Antonia Brico: "She has the most beautiful hands I have ever seen. They are huge and smooth and strong. The fingers are long and the veins are all in the right places, like a Rodin sculpture." [*The Judy Collins Songbook*]

The atmosphere at Dr. Brico's studio was a grave, imposing one for a young girl. The busts of classical composers and conductors stared down at her. She worked hard, perhaps too hard for a child. Everyone assumed she would become a concert pianist because she was so gifted.

But something was going wrong for Judy. Although her music training was progressing, her teenage years were miserable the way only those years can be. The discipline of constant piano practice contributed to her problems. She felt friendless, cut off from a social life. She knew how to play the piano, but she didn't know how to *play.*

She had worries common to many teenage girls. She was self-conscious about being flat-chested, and was anxious to develop physically. She slept with a clothespin on her nose, hoping it would alter its shape and make it smaller. She was very inhibited, shy in public, afraid to dance. Even though she had friends, she didn't really feel like part of a group.

She began to fight with her parents over practicing the piano. She fought especially with her father, who had begun to pressure her. They fought seriously over a Liszt piece called *Campanella,* which her father wanted her to play at a program he was doing, and which Judy insisted she wasn't ready for. The fight was an extended one and Judy became more and more depressed. Finally she was so unhappy she made a half-hearted suicide attempt. She didn't really mean to kill herself, but was trying like many who try suicide unsuccessfully, to give a signal that the pressures were too great.

So one day when she was sixteen she went to Dr. Brico's studio and said she didn't want to continue playing the piano. It was an emotional scene, with Dr. Brico trying to persuade the talented young musician that the sacrifices to be a concert pianist were worth it. But Judy was adamant. She was giving up piano. Her heart was no longer in it.

Quitting piano was not an easy decision. It left a vacuum in Judy's life. Secretly she knew she could not escape her connection to music.

Then Judy Collins got her first guitar. She had heard a man named Lingo the Drifter play the guitar at her house, and was fascinated. Her father, happy to see Judy interested in music again, gave her a guitar and lessons for her next birthday.

At her first lesson she realized the man who was supposed to teach her was not very instructive for her. She decided to teach herself, from records. She would listen to records, learn the songs, and then search out the tunes on the guitar. Eventually she met people who played and who taught her in a helpful way.

Playing the guitar allowed her to continue with music but did not isolate her from people the way classical piano had, with its long, rigorous hours of solitary practice. Guitar drew people closer to her. She would play and everybody would sing. Many of her social problems disappeared.

In a high school writing class she had a disastrous experience with writing, which blocked her about writing, another field she is very talented in, for many years. She wrote a paper on T. S. Eliot, a poet she often discussed with her father, and her teacher accused her of plagiarizing it. When Judy denied it, the teacher didn't believe her. Judy had to call in another writing teacher she'd studied with, who said she was capable of very fine work. But the damage was done. It was eight or ten years before she did serious writing again.

When Judy finished high school she worked in a guest ranch in the mountains for the summer, and in the fall entered Mac-Murray College in Illinois, where she had a scholarship. The year she spent in college was a miserable one. When she returned to Denver she did a perfectly natural thing. She married her childhood sweetheart, Peter.

Peter was three years older than Judy and was working on his doctorate in English literature. Judy loved literature and loved Peter and felt secure. During their first married summer Peter and Judy got a job running a lodge in the wilderness of Rocky

Mountain National Park. They had to walk in with backpacks, and most of the supplies were brought in by pack horse to their lodge near the timberline. Judy baked breads in a wood stove and played guitar and sang in the evenings. It was a beautiful, idyllic summer.

Looking back, Judy Collins understands she was too young to be married. She didn't know herself well enough. She sensed that someday she would grow away from Peter. But in those days, in the fifties, a woman could not simply live with a man—marriage was the only way to be together. And during the idyllic summer in the Rocky Mountains Judy found that she was pregnant.

They moved back to Boulder in the fall and Peter returned to school. Judy worked at the university to help support them and prepared to be a mother. In January her son Clark was born, a red-haired, blue-eyed baby.

It was Peter's idea that she get a job singing. Judy went to a local beer joint called Michael's Pub and auditioned. She was hired to sing in the evenings for $100 a week. It was 1959, and at 19, she was beginning her professional career as a singer.

Soon her reputation spread and she got a higher-paying job in nearby Central City, but she was away from Peter and Clark more than she wanted to be.

Leaving a husband, a marriage, is not easy, nor is it usually rapid. Though turmoil was growing inside Judy Collins, she moved with Peter and Clark to Chicago for the summer. There she sang at the Gate of Horn. Her experience and repertoire were growing.

Then they moved to Connecticut, where Peter had a teaching job, and Judy began commuting to Boston to sing at a club called the Golden Vanity. She also began to tour in Canada. Each trip, each acknowledgement of her growing professional involvement with music, took her farther from her life with Peter. Part of her wanted to be a university wife, but the part of her that was a singer was stronger.

Then Jac Holzman of Elektra Records heard her sing at Gerde's Folk City in New York and signed her to record. In October 1961 she made her first album, *A Maid of Constant Sorrow,* and eight months later cut her second, *Golden Apples of the Sun.* At the end of the summer, after cutting her second record, Judy told Peter she was going to leave him.

Shortly thereafter, Judy played her first Carnegie Hall concert as Theodore Bikel's guest. Her parents came from Denver to see her and sat, proud and moved, in the first row.

After the Carnegie Hall concert Judy flew to Tucson to sing, and while she was there saw a doctor about the pain in her chest. She had tuberculosis. She was in the hospital in Tucson for a month, sick and alone. She tried comforting herself by studying guitar, improving her technique. Then she was transferred to the National Jewish Hospital in Denver, where she spent another four months. Clark was still in her custody, staying with Judy's mother, but Peter came and took him to Connecticut. The divorce was going through. Judy had made her choice, and when she was well enough to travel, she went to New York.

When she reached New York she made *Judy Collins #3* and began to receive national attention as a folksinger. Like other folksingers, she believed in political commitment. Her third album had been released in March 1964, and the following August she went down to Mississippi, where many people were working on voter registration drives. The racism of the white Southerners, the atmosphere of hatred and fear, made for an extremely intense experi-

Jim Marshall

13

ence, and increased her sense of the importance of political commitment.

However, at the end of that summer Judy's personal life interfered with her career, with her entire sense of herself, on a new scale. She lost custody of Clark. One of the reasons the court decided against her was because she was seeing a psychoanalyst. It seemed that she was being penalized for trying to grow as a person.

Losing Clark was a shattering experience. At first she was numb, and simply continued with her concerts, her music. But soon after losing custody she was scheduled to give a concert in Grand Junction, Colorado. In a hotel room there, for the first time in her life, she broke down badly. At the hour she was supposed to perform, she boarded a plane back to New York.

It was the beginning of living with tremendous grief. She felt numb a great deal. She drove to Connecticut to see Clark whenever she could. Peter remarried and had another child, and the situation was complicated for Clark, who could not understand why he was separated from his mother.

Judy developed violent headaches and a bad stomach. She felt lost, uncertain, while groping her way, working hard in

analysis. Slowly she rediscovered how central her music was to her. It was her strength, her center. She produced albums regularly, and her taste in music changed, becoming less political. Music became a way of personally connecting with people. It helped make up for the loss of Clark.

In 1966 Judy suffered another loss. Her close friend Richard Farina was killed in a motorcycle accident, the night of the party to celebrate publication of his first novel, *Been Down So Long It Looks Like Up to Me.* Farina, who at the time of his death was married to Mimi Baez and who before that had been married to Carolyn Hester, has become a kind of legend. He was an extraordinary man whose friends loved him deeply.

Judy first met Richard Farina at a music festival early in her singing career. The festival was in Indian Neck, Connecticut, and most folksingers she had ever heard of were present. One prized moment was hearing the Rev. Gary Davis sing. Judy's friend Carolyn Hester, who at that time was the queen of the folk music scene, was there with her husband Dick Farina. Judy was drawn to his intensity, found herslef almost frightened of this wild, warm man with the dark, laughing eyes. She sang for him and Carolyn in their

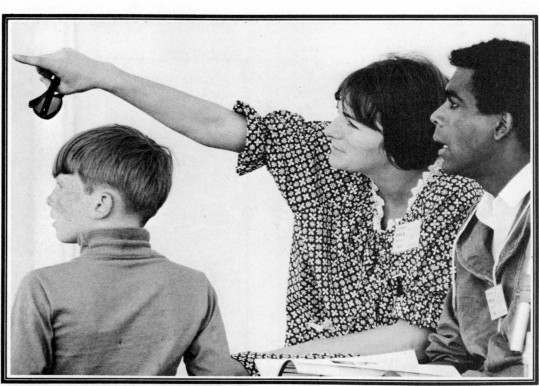

David Gahr. Judy with Clark Taylor and Bill Lee, Newport Folk Festival, 1960

hotel room, and a serious friendship between her and Dick was formed.

Years later she visited him on Martha's Vineyard. He had just begun to write his novel, but was also writing songs and poems. She was moved by his work and the friendship deepened.

She saw him again in Monterey at a music festival, after he had married Mimi Baez. Dick and Mimi sang and played for her, Dick on the dulcimer and Mimi on guitar. Their magical songs together have become well known now, part of Richard Farina's legacy.

Then Richard and Mimi moved to Cambridge, and Judy saw them frequently. Richard had been a major source of support and comfort in the difficult custody case over Clark. On her *Fifth Album* Richard plays the dulcimer. He wrote a long poem for Judy that is reprinted on the cover.

Then, in May 1966, came his tragic death. The loss matured Judy, helped prepare her for her father's death, which followed shortly. However, between the deaths of her friend and her father, a wonderful thing happened to Judy Collins, a healing, nurturing thing that centered her and enabled her to live with loss.

In 1967 her son Clark told his father

Jim Marshall. Mr and Mrs Collins

that he wanted to live with his mother. After some negotiating, Peter agreed to give Clark up. They worked out the arrangements, and since then, Clark his lived with Judy. Although nothing can completely erase the terrible grief and the loss of those years with her son, Judy has found it marvelously rewarding to be with her child. A teenager now, he is also a musician and has gone on the road with his own band.

Not long after Clark was returned to her, Judy's father died. He had been badly depressed and Judy had sent her parents to Honolulu for a vacation. While they were there her father got sick. The doctors were not sure what was wrong with him then, nor after he was returned to Denver were they really able to determine the problem. Judy was embittered by her father's death. She felt that he had simply given up his will to live, that he wanted to die, and she felt rejected, angry, and guilty. She has written about her father and his attitude toward anger. She feels she learned anger from him and that it was a valuable lesson. "Specifically I think the most important thing I could say about that is to tell you that I'm learning to get my anger out at the time it happens. . . . Anger's part of one's life. I always tell my kid. . . if he feels anger towards somebody, they deserve to have that anger given to them because it belongs to them. And if he covers it up, and tucks it someplace where it's going to rot in him, then he's also done them a disservice. There's nothing wrong with anger . . . anger is a very important outlet." (Monica Bay, *Minnesota Daily,* November 2, 1973)

Judy's mother did a beautiful thing at her father's funeral. She refused to let anyone wear black. She said Judy's father wouldn't have wanted anyone to. And her mother has continued with her own independent life.

After Clark was returned to her, Judy fixed up her apartment and settled into a comfortable, growing life. She lives in a spacious, high-ceilinged apartment on the Upper West Side in Manhattan. Its rooms are warm and well decorated without being self-consciously sophisticated. There is a beautiful view of the Hudson, with panoramic sunsets each evening. The nine rooms are filled with pianos, a cut-down organ, guitars, records, plants, books, and four cats.

As Judy has become more famous and more comfortable with herself and with her

David Gahr. With Stacey Keach at Arlo Guthrie's wedding, 1969

life, she has become more private. In a way she seems to have mastered the art of being private in public. It is known, for instance, that she lived for years with the actor Stacy Keach. Their relationship was so permanent that they often joked that they were married, though they had no intention of marriage. Neither of them believed in it. One wonders what happened, since in 1974 they split up and Keach suddenly married Marilyn Aiken.

We also know that Judy had a year-long involvement with Stephen Stills, of the rock group Crosby, Stills, Nash and Young. Stills wrote "Suite: Judy Blue Eyes" for her. Yet it is not easy to find out more about Judy's love life. She surrounds herself with friends and privacy. She does not wish to have her private life smeared across the media, and in fact is not interested in the larger-than-life image many musicians want to project. Robin Katz (*Sounds,* June 7, 1975) asked Judy to comment on the difference in her own image and the public images of Joan Baez and Joni Mitchell. Katz noted the tendency of music stars to stand on a pedestal. Judy said, "Stars make their own images. They create around them what they want and I happen to want different things. Joni may want to feel that way, both Baez and

Mitchell. Dylan and the McCartneys may feel that way. For me there's nothing in it. I really believe that one creates an aura around oneself and you can pick it and choose it. You can choose to have no friends and be extremely isolated. You can look like the poor waif. Or you can choose something else."

Judy Collins has certainly chosen something else. She has chosen to be private about her life, she has chosen to have friends and to trust them, and she has chosen to be a star in what can only be described as an unassuming way. There is a simplicity, a straight-forwardness about Judy Collins that is very touching, and there is a humility about her that is genuine.

She does talk often about her relationship with her son Clark. For the first year after Clark was returned to her they spent their time feeling each other out. Each of them was insecure—Clark naturally afraid he would be separated from Judy again, and Judy afraid she would be a disappointment to her son. Judy did not feel that Clark was being deprived of a father, an objection that is commonly raised when it comes to male children living with divorced mothers. She felt it was clear that Clark *had* a father and that she was not depriving him. Aware of the

Nancy Dubin. Clark Taylor, Tanglewood Concert, 1975

generation gap, she tried to raise Clark the way she would like to have been raised. If something important came up between them—and this is still true—they would talk about it. She has always wanted Clark to be a musician, but has been careful not to push him in the ways she was pushed. Recently he has begun to tour with his own band, and Judy was surprised to find she felt some fear for him, some loss, ambivalence as well as pride. She has written beautifully of her reactions in the song "Born to the Breed."

Totally resisting society's pressures to marry and provide Clark with a father, refusing to marry Stacy Keach and trying to maintain a relationship with him that would not be restrictive for either of them, trying first and always to be herself, Judy has become very conscious of her role in society as a woman. She told Gloria Steinem on a television show that she had outgrown the need for a "prince charming." She has become an ardent feminist though certainly not a strident one. She always emphasizes the humanist aspect of feminism. Her friendships with men are important to her, just as her relationships with her son and her brothers are important to her.

One man whose friendship has been vital to Judy Collins is Leonard Cohen. She

met him by accident through friends, and he played "Suzanne" for her and "Dress Rehearsal Rag." She recognized his amazing talent immediately, and both songs went into her sixth album. She was largely responsible for bringing Cohen's haunting work to the public eye. Since Cohen's voice is not the best, it took the crystalline loveliness of a voice like Judy Collins' to make the public see his greatness as a poet and songwriter.

Another man whose friendship has been essential to Collins is Max Margulis, her voice teacher. Collins' integrity and humility are demonstrated by the fact that even now, as a superstar, she still takes voice lessons. Margulis' methods are unorthodox. He is not particularly interested in scales, breath control, or other mechanical problems of singing. What he insists upon is concentration, a sort of Zen approach to singing. He urges Collins to *become* the narrator of the song she is singing. If she is feeling the lyrics completely, then the audience will feel them too.

The effect of studying voice has been tremendous. When Collins recorded her first few albums, she was an alto. "In those days I was a very untrained singer, and I

was literally using about the lower third of my voice all the time because I didn't know that there was anything up there." (Susan Elliott, *High Fidelity,* April 1977.) Now her voice has the earthy, husky sound of the alto that was her original stock-in-trade, as well as something that reaches far beyond that into a lovely, ethereal, pure soprano.

Partly thanks to Margulis' wonderful teaching, Judy has become more and more what might best be described as an actress while she is singing. She makes us believe in the *content* of the song, the storytelling part of it. She seems to *become* the young girl who dreams of following her rodeo-riding boyfriend in "Someday Soon." She becomes the voice of blind justice in her chilling rendition of "Pretty Polly." In

"Simple Gifts" she seems astoundingly innocent. She follows Margulis' cryptic advice: the music is already out there, you only have to find it.

Judy Collins loves getting older because as she matures the range of her accomplishments has broadened. Her audience is changing too. No longer is it just teenagers who love her singing—she draws fans of all ages, from all different types of lives.

Judy's philosophy is based on work. She believes in her inborn talent for music and is now grateful for the encouragement her parents gave her. But she also believes that one has a responsibility to one's talents, and she has worked long and hard to develop hers to the fullest.

19

Her Career,
Accomplishments,
& Politics

Sheldon Ramsdell: Anti-war demonstration, Washington, 1972

3.

Judy Collins is more than a singer, more than a songwriter, more than a brilliant interpreter of others' songs. She is intensely political without being narrow-minded, and she has a range of interests that reaches beyond music. Her most famous recent accomplishment, perhaps eclipsing her albums, is her film, *Antonia: A Portrait of the Woman,* which she produced and co-directed. The film is made with the courage, intelligence, and taste that run through Collins' work and life. But in order to understand how Collins' multitalents bloomed when the careers of so many others have withered, we must go back through her life to see the way politics and other interests contributed and mixed in with her music.

It is important to remember that Collins did not start out to be a singer. Her early training was as a concert pianist. Withdrawing from classical piano because she felt isolated, she started folk music as a hobby. When it turned into a living, she became one of a large group of folksingers emerging across the country, changing the face of American music.

She got her start in the early sixties, when folk music was first becoming popular with the middle class and, hence, commercial and respectable. There was the hit television show "Hootenanny," and the fashionable groups of the time—the Kingston Trio

and Peter, Paul, and Mary. There were lesser-known folksingers too, who were not as commercially successful but perhaps ultimately more important: Bruce Langhorne and the Rev. Gary Davis and Bob Gibson and Richard Farina and Carolyn Hester. Then these figures gave way to the prime movers in folk music: Bob Dylan and Joan Baez and Judy Collins.

Of all these figures, Judy Collins is the only one who actually extended the folk music framework, partly through her own fine writing; partly by bringing to the forefront contemporary folk artists like Leonard Cohen, Jacques Brel, and Joni Mitchell; partly by popularizing such nonmainstream songs as "Send in the Clowns" and "Amazing Grace."

Judy Collins is no longer comfortable with the label "folksinger," and yet the label clings. In a way, what Judy sings *becomes* folk music.

Not only did Collins start out as something other than a singer, but she was not political when she first started, either. She had always been interested in folk music, but didn't actually know what it was. But even while she was still playing classical piano, when she and some friends heard "The Gypsy Rover" on the radio, they made a little skit out of it, which they choreographed and performed.

It was after she'd quit piano that Judy met Lingo the Drifter, a folksinger and storyteller whom her father brought home one night. Lingo sang songs by Pete Seeger and the Weavers and Woody Guthrie. He not only introduced Judy to folk music, he introduced her to the folk music world. As Collins told *High Fidelity,* Lingo and his entourage "would get together and sing, drink beer, and carry on to all hours of the night." (Susan Elliott, April 1977.)

When Judy began playing guitar at 16, she won a Kiwanis Club singing contest and was sent to Atlantic City, New Jersey, to perform in the hall where the Miss America contest was held. Facing an enormous room filled with people in Kiwanis hats eating popcorn from the boardwalk, it was an inauspicious beginning.

Judy Collins was very naive in those years. She was popular in her first engage-

milieu was such that simply being a folksinger was to be political. Our major folksingers were trying desperately to wake America up to its injustice. Judy, like the others, really believed that she had a moral responsibility as a singer.

These were the years when Judy went to Mississippi to help with voter registration. These were the years when, at the Chicago Seven Trial, she rose in the witness box and sang "Where Have All the Flowers Gone," in reply to the prosecutor's questions. Those were the years she became involved in the Women's Strike for Peace. In 1967 she coproduced, with Ethel Raim of the Pennywhistlers, an album called *Save the*

Jim Marshall. Judy's first concert with Dylan, 1962

Jim Marshall. With Eric Weissberg, New York, 1963

ments in Boulder, Denver, and Chicago, but she had no interest in stardom. She was working to support her husband and child. When she began playing the folk circuit, including Greenwich Village, she became more professional about her music, but still had no comprehension of her growing popularity. When Jac Holzman, then president of Elektra Records, offered her a recording contract, she was shocked. She was sure she wasn't ready.

The material in *A Maid of Constant Sorrow* and *Golden Apples of the Sun* is mostly public-domain folk. However, in her next three albums she included work by Richard Farina, Bob Dylan, Woody Guthrie, Gordon Lightfoot, and Phil Ochs.

Those were political times. The social

Children in connection with the Women's Strike. *Save the Children* contained songs and recitations by Judy, Joan Baez, Mimi Farina, Janis Ian, Odetta, Viveca Lindfors, and the Pennywhistlers.

During that time, Judy's music was undergoing a transformation. She had realized that folksingers like herself were singing heavy political music to people who already agreed with them. There was a kind of closed circuit going on. And she began to feel restricted by the musical nature of the protest work. Most protest songs are not really folk songs. Their function is like a newspaper's: attempts to inform people. Often that function imposes limits on how interesting those songs are musically. Judy's interest, her taste, was growing be-

David Gahr. With Theo Bikel, Newport Folk Festival, 1963

Jim Marshall. Big Sur Folk Festival, 1966—Joan Baez and Mimi Farina

Jim Marshall. Newport Folk Festival, 1966

yond simple folk music.

In 1966 she did *In My Life,* marking a substantial change in her musical approach. She and her producer Mark Abramson had decided to do more theatrical pieces. So *In My Life* contains a Brecht song, but also introduces Leonard Cohen ("Suzanne," "Dress Rehearsal Rag") as well as the now-famous songwriters Jacques Brel and Randy Newman. This new material required more sophisticated orchestrations, so Judy worked with Joshua Rifkin, who at that time was associated with Nonesuch, Elektra's classical label. The classical strain was slowly coming back into her work. And

her own personal pleasure and development as an artist.

Yet Judy Collins' work has consisted, in a way, of a dialectic between her political self and her artistic self. The two strains of her character sometimes battle each other but more often nourish each other. It was terribly important to her career that she moved away from simple protest music. Yet, in the late sixties, when she seemed to move away from political work too completely, she became divided.

Judy has always been interested in acting, another aspect of her multi-faceted career. Although her concerts have some-

David Gahr. With Ritchie Havens, Pete Seeger and Bill Lee, Carnegie Hall, 1968

there were other signs that, musically, she was beginning to flex into something closer to her full range: *In My Life* was her first gold album.

Judy was recognizing that she was not an evangelist—she was an entertainer, a performer. She could separate her political self from her music, at least in some contexts. She was not a strident politico, but a humanist. Especially after her son Clark was returned to her, it seemed important to be less urgent, not to try to solve the world's problems overnight, and to clear space for

times been subtle acting performances, in the summer of 1969 she had her official acting debut, playing Solveig in a Central Park production of Henrik Ibsen's *Peer Gynt.* She seemed idyllically happy that summer —acting with Stacy Keach, riding bicycles to the park for performances. And she loved the songs in the production.

What hung in the background of this idyll was the Vietnam War. Judy was looking for some personal solution. Her personal happiness was so great that she convinced herself it was possible to opt out, to look for a hideaway. It was during this period that Dan Berrigan called her, before the Catonsville action. He wanted her to do a benefit. Collins later told *Crawdaddy* interviewer Peter Knobler (October 1972) how she had said, "I really can't, you know." And Berrigan replied, "It's so hard for me to talk to you, to accept your . . . your reticence when my own consciousness of how serious this is is so great."

At this time Judy was producing some of her most brilliant records, which rarely contained any overt political material. *Who Knows Where the Times Goes,* perhaps her

thinks war is insane, and so, when she went to Paris, it was with her mind already made up. Nevertheless, meeting with the Vietnamese peace delegation was a shocking, radicalizing experience. The *reality* of the war came home to her. She could see the North Vietnamese as human beings, not as abstractions, and she came to love and respect them. Many people told her that the Vietnamese were propagandizing, but she didn't buy that objection. She felt closer to them, she shared a sense of the importance of humanism with them. At the American Embassy, on the other hand, she and the

David Gahr. Judy, Pete Seeger, Bob Dylan and Arlo Guthrie, Carnegie Hall, 1968

most wonderful album, was from this period, as were *Recollections* and *Whales and Nightingales.* She told herself that there was no such thing as a political song, that all songs were political. Yet her unease grew.

Then in 1971 she went on a fact-finding mission to Paris, to meet some of the Vietnamese. From this trip, her political nature flared up, more permanently now, and more mature and focused than in the days of her early protest songs, her early marches and actions.

Judy has always been against war. She

others in her group were treated coldly, almost with suspicion. She told Peter Knobler (*Crawdaddy,* October 1972): "It was a frightening kind of trip for me in a lot of ways because I felt very disembodied and very spaced by the whole thing, and kind of in shock throughout the whole experience."

Judy still believes that the "peace" achieved in Vietnam is disgraceful. Since we tried to destroy that country and came very close to doing so, we are left in this country with an indelible sense of guilt, of having done wrong. Some kind of repara-

Camera 5

27

tion, some kind of reckoning, will be necessary, not just financial but moral as well.

At any rate, Judy was repoliticized by meeting with the Vietnamese. She no longer felt that she had the option of nonparticipation. She campaigned hard for McGovern in his disastrous run for the Presidency. She also campaigned for U.S. Congresswoman Pat Schroeder from Colorado, who, unlike McGovern, won her election. She was not simply trying to work "through the system," though. She was aware of the need for more direct action. She appeared regularly at peace marches and civil rights demonstrations all through the sixties, despite her temporary withdrawals from politics. In 1972 she was busted for blocking the halls of Congress. She also became involved in prison reform work.

Judy believes that supporting local election candidates is especially important. She is aware of the fact that much progress is stopped not only by the executive branch of the government, but by antiquated representatives and senators as well. It costs a lot of money to run for office, and asking enter-

tainers to do benefits both raises money and generates publicity.

She told Alanna Nash (*Sounds,* March 9, 1974): "Most performers are trying to make some dent in the people who listen to them; they try to express themselves in ways that will encourage people to vote in a different way or think in a different way, to stop behaving as if war were the only solution to humanity's problems."

What is crucial here is that Judy, when she returned to political action after her brief and partial withdrawal in the late sixties, did not confuse singing political music with being political. She had matured in several different ways.

She asked *Crawdaddy*'s Peter Knobler: "What would you do if you could do something that would gain attention immediately only because of people recognizing your name or knowing you?" Judy recognizes the importance of her own fame, knows it has automatic power, and does not take that power for granted. She wants to use her fame without being pigeonholed, because that would render her ineffective. Hence

Nancy Dubin Central Park, New York, 1973

28

she tries to present herself directly, in all her complexity, without oversimplifying her views.

That she was able to work in electoral politics at a time when many disenchanted Americans were limiting themselves to more radical actions is an indication of her maturity and the breadth of her humanist vision.

Another strong element in Judy's politics has been her continual concern with prison reform. She became involved in prison work almost by accident. She was in Alabama to see the filming of a prison being torn down, as she was to sing a Dylan song for the soundtrack of the film. She was horrified by the prison, found it hard to believe that people actually had lived there. Grim reminders that people *had* lived there could be seen in personal effects left behind in the cells by the inmates, who had never been told they were being moved. As Judy told Alanna Nash in *Sounds,* "This place was really the most awful place I've ever been in my life, and I've been in some pretty awful places."

The film of this, *The Repeater,* shows how prisoners are made dependent on society and how this becomes a vicious circle they are unable to break out of. In Alabama, for instance, prisoners were given $10 upon release, with which they were supposed to go out into the world and reestablish themselves. They were in an impossible situation.

Dylan refused use of his song for the soundtrack, so Judy co-authored one with Stacy Keach called "Easy Times." Judy has strong feelings about what happens to those on the outside who love prisoners, and she had seen a lot of correspondence between male prisoners and their wives and girlfriends. So she wrote the song from the point of view of a woman whose man is in prison.

Judy has sung in prisons several times, and plans at some point to do a prison tour. One aspect of such concerts that has meant a lot to her is that prison audiences are racially integrated, and Judy doesn't often get to reach black people. Her commercial audiences are primarily white.

She told Peter Knobler about playing at Danbury prison while the Berrigans were still confined there: "There were lots and lots of black prisoners who came and stayed through the concert, which I thought was wonderful. I mean, I have very little way to reach a black audience, really. Most of my audience, like most white performers, is pretty much a white audience. I don't like it but I don't know what exactly to do about it . . . ."

Judy has always felt that the best thing she could do was simply be herself, rather than try artificially to bridge a cultural gap. She felt that the Danbury concert allowed that to happen. The black men *liked* her music.

Racism has concerned Judy her entire adult life, and she has been politically active about it since 1964 when she went to Mississippi to help with voter registration.

In the early seventies Judy spent a lot of time trying to help free Michael Malik, who then was a black power leader in England and a friend of Judy's. Michael Malik was hanged in Trinidad, and Judy believes that he was framed. She believes a deal was made to get rid of him because he was organizing the black West Indians in England.

In discussing her political involvements, Judy told interviewer Robert Weinstein: "I think of life as a political process. The way one handles love and hate, one to one, is a reflection of how one handles it politically . . . . So there is always the personal political situation which I feel very strongly about, whether it is becoming oneself as a woman or becoming oneself as a voice against something. Politics has vast scope and covers all our relationships with one another."

Judy has always been working from a sense that what is personal is political and vice versa. That she should become involved with the women's movement, where "the personal is political," is a natural development. Before looking at her feminism, however, we must go back and look at another way she was maturing in these years: in her writing.

In 1969 she told journalist Barbara Rowes, "Finally after all these years of looking for the beautiful songs that I could sing, wanted to sing, I started to write my own songs, and that is completely different. Paul Simon told me it straightens out your head, and he is right."

She had begun trying to write earlier, in 1966, the year before her son Clark was returned to her. She started keeping a notebook, in the hope that it would generate songs. She knew other writers who worked this way. However, this method was not successful for her. Whenever she thought of a line or an image she would write it down, but she was painfully shy about her notebook, could not show it to anyone, and her work in it was fragmented.

Finally she showed the notebook to her friend Bruce Langhorne. He found the material too dark and brooding, and instead of working with the notebook told her to write five songs about relationships between men and women. Her first song came in a 1½-hour burst: "Since You Asked," which was recorded on the album *Wildflowers.* Breaking through to writing a song was so intense for her it made her cry.

She wrote three songs for the *Wildflowers* album, then slowed down and produced only six songs in five years. However, during that time she also wrote poems and several articles, and a lot of autobiographical material for *The Judy Collins Songbook.*

Then, in 1973, her album *True Stories and Other Dreams* was released, with five of her own songs, the first album comprised substantially of her original material. She made it clear, however, that she did not intend to become a songwriter, did not consider it a goal to write all her own songs. She told Susan Elliott (*High Fidelity,* April 1977): "I have a career on many different levels . . . it would be very limiting for me to do all my own material. I think a lot of singers who have to write their own are constantly faced with a tremendous and difficult obstacle to overcome. There are a few people who have come through that way over the years, but it's very hard."

Judy has great respect for the *process* of writing. She knows from her own experience what great concentration is required, how much writing depends on being true to your own vision of things, and that writing is a gift.

In 1972, when she went to her Grandmother Byrd's funeral in Seattle, part of her aim was to take a look at her roots. She had been born in Seattle, and had spent her first years there. She told Peter Knobler: "I saw the house on the corner, and the street, and I was *stunned,* because it's so little . . . . There's nothing! It's a dumb little house on a corner in Seattle. But in my head it is the most lush, florid, vivid, sensual, pleasurable, complicated, marvelous place in the world. In my memory. In my imagination. And I realized as we went by that *nobody knows that but me."*

Judy wrote a wonderful article for *Ms.* magazine in the April 1973 issue in which she describes this trip to Seattle and how it

eventually led her to write the song "Secret Gardens of the Heart." This trip to Seattle was an epiphany that brought out the integrity of her own vision, and she turned that epiphany into art.

Judy often collaborates—more accurately, shares a mutually nourishing work space—with her friend poet Cynthia MacDonald. They often work in the same room, helping each other concentrate, supporting each other, and consoling each other over the difficulties of writing.

In 1972 Judy Collins, at the height of her career, seemed to retire from music.

Actually she had not retired at all, but had simply shifted directions again. She was producing and co-directing her brilliant documentary movie *Antonia: A Portrait of the Woman.*

Searching for her roots again, Judy had planned originally to return to Denver and interview Dr. Brico, her childhood music teacher, for an article in *Ms.* A friend suggested she film the interview. Rather than make a "home movie," Collins contacted filmmaker Jill Godmilow, who

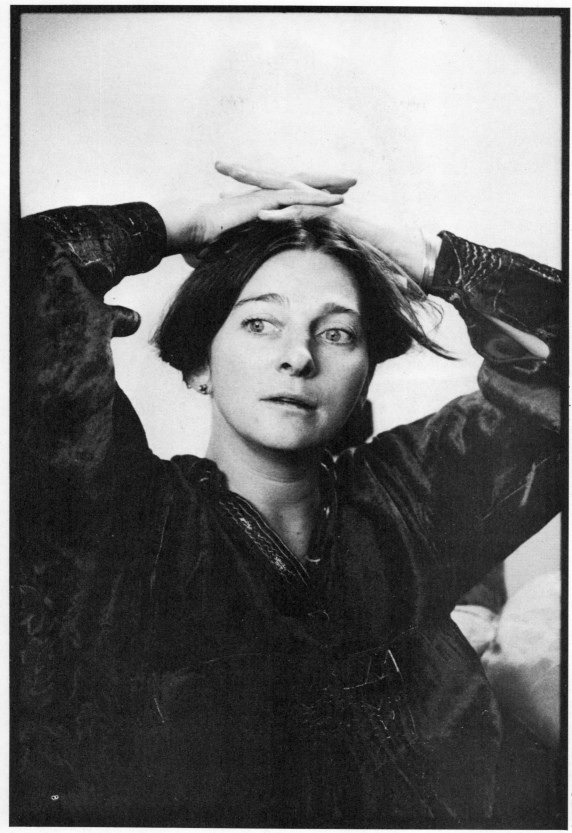

Joseph Stevens, London, 1973

directed and edited the picture. The scope of the project rapidly grew. It soon became clear that Antonia Brico was a fabulous subject for a documentary.

Collins was becoming more involved with the feminist movement. She had joined a consciousness-raising group which had a tremendous effect on her. Judy thought that getting in touch with Dr. Brico and her extraordinary life would help her build her own courage, would give her affirmation to make her own way in the world. In filming Dr. Brico, she not only did something important for the external world and the women's movement, she also did something important for herself.

One result of producing *Antonia* was that she left Harold Leventhal to become her own manager. The parting was amicable and Leventhal still produces her New York concerts. Collins formed her own company, Rocky Mountain Productions. She financed the film independently, so that she and Godmilow and Brico could have total control of the final product. Once again, Collins' integrity paid off.

Leventhal had the reputation of protecting Collins' privacy. Judy was afraid she would not make it on her own. The feminist movement was showing her the ways in which she depended on men, and the ways in which that dependency limited her. Making the film not only freed her from her overdependence on male producers, it also freed her from her overdependence on her long-time lover Stacy Keach. Producing *Antonia* had a profound effect on Judy Collins' life.

Antonia: A Portrait of the Woman opened in 1974 to rave reviews. It was chosen to open the American Filmmakers Series at the Whitney Museum, has played commercially in New York and Los Angeles, and has been shown nationally on television. Along the way the film has been named one of the top ten films of 1974 by *Time* magazine, has won the Christopher Award, the Independent Film Critics Award, Mlle. Award, and was nominated for an Academy Award as the best documentary of 1974.

The film gave Judy a rare chance to combine her feminist politics with her extraordinary sensitivity as an artist. It also allowed her to pay loving tribute to her early and influential teacher. Judy feels that *Antonia* is the most important political statement she has made. Her conviction that the personal is political runs through the film,

even though there is no mention of politics at all. Yet the film is about the effects of sex discrimination on Antonia Brico.

The film traces the efforts of Dr. Brico to become a conductor. She was first taught piano as a child because she bit her nails. An enormous natural talent and a tremendous dedication to music soon revealed themselves in the young girl. She formed the ambition of becoming a conductor, but conducting was a man's field. Antonia was constantly told that it was ridiculous for her to try to break into conducting. She says in the film, "I felt that I'd never forgive myself if I didn't try."

In her twenties she was known worldwide as the first woman conductor. Yet there was a patronizing quality in critical reaction to her, as if what was extraordinary about her was not her talent as a conductor but the simple fact that she was a woman. Art may be sexless, as Dr. Brico asserts, but the world did not treat her as if this were so. A typical patronizing comment was her *New York Times* headline in 1930: **Yankee Girl Startles Berlin Critics.**

After her triumph in Europe, Dr. Brico directed the Metropolitan Opera. However, she was denied a third concert because John Charles Thomas, the baritone, refused to work with a woman conductor.

She tried a different tactic: between 1934 and 1937, she formed and conducted a women's symphony. The women's symphony thrived, and Dr. Brico thought she had firmly established women's competence in classical music.

Then she tried to convert it into a symphony of both men and women. The board of directors of Carnegie Hall rejected the project, saying that it was undramatic. "I want people," Dr. Brico says, "to mix in symphonies as they do in life." There was no forum for such a radical idea.

In the forties her career began to decline. She had been a sensational novelty, but the world would not allow Antonia Brico to simply develop as a serious conductor.

In the film, Dr. Brico is ebullient, warm, honest. She asserts that she is happy in Denver, with friends and students who love and admire her. Yet one night while cleaning up her kitchen she confides to interviewer Collins, "I don't talk about it every day. I don't let everyone know my heartbreak."

It is the film's most moving scene, as

Dr. Brico reveals her anguish over not being allowed to conduct. She conducts only five times a year, although she has the energy to do much more. She explains that a soloist can play a piece for herself, for her own enjoyment, but a conductor needs the whole orchestra and the audience. She says, "I cannot play my instrument, which is the orchestra."

Such intensely personal revelations are rare in film, and it is a tribute to Collins' sensitivity, the atmosphere of trust she establishes with Dr. Brico in the film, that she was able to capture such a poignant moment.

The film is low-key and intimate and conscientious. The method allows Dr. Brico herself to carry the film, and to assert her own style in it. There is no chronological structure to the film. Collins and Godmilow simply weave a tapestry of sequences showing Brico at work with her orchestra in Denver, going about her present life, with reminiscences about her good friends like Artur Rubinstein and Albert Schweitzer, old newspaper clippings and newsreels and memories which slowly and surely reveal the brilliant promise of her career and the sex discrimination that limited its development.

The only intrusion by the filmmakers into the story itself consists of one brief animated sequence called the "Great Kettledrum War of 1937," which portrays an instrumental combat between Brico's drummer and a male counterpart. The sequence lends a light, fantasy touch to this seriously wonderful movie.

Dr. Brico herself surpasses this good-humored element later in the film when she sits down at her piano and bangs out some jazz pieces, singing them in her own version of a vaudeville belter's voice. After she's finished singing, she says, "I'm not so sure I want that public, dear." We feel grateful for the way in which this proud, fiery woman has opened her heart on film and told her story.

One unexpected effect of the film's widespread success has been to stimulate Antonia Brico's career. Although she is now in her seventies, she has been offered many new chances to conduct. Dr. Brico has risen to the opportunities, and her work has been acclaimed both here and in Europe. Nevertheless, she has managed to keep all of her pupils in Denver as well as her orchestra there. She is an amazing and loyal woman.

Judy Collins' commitment to feminism is not a head trip. It seems to come from her core, from her center. She told Monica Bay (*Minnesota Daily*) in 1973: "I think it's an important aspect of all of our lives because it has something to do with the whole culture. What's going on in politics . . . every part of the world is deeply affected by the feminist movement."

She is careful to emphasize that she is not anti-male. She has sometimes said that she wishes the feminist movement were called the humanist movement, because she believes that men will benefit from it as much as women. "It must be hideous to have to walk around with an erection all the time—to get it up, and get it on; keep it up, keep succeeding, keep being the big, tough, macho person. Who needs it?"

Certainly she doesn't. Her politics are reflected in the way she runs her own company, as well as in the fact that she has taken over management of her own career. She told Susan Elliott (*High Fidelity,* April 1977): "I don't want to have somebody take my life and run it . . . appear when and where they say I should. I have a need to guide my own life . . . with professional help. People tend to categorize themselves as either artists or business people. My own feeling is that there's always a lot of overlap, and if you're responsible, then you can take care of your own business."

Rocky Mountain Productions has three male employees and three female, and decisions are made cooperatively. Judy believes there are parallels in the different aspects of her life. She thinks that filmmaking has a musical quality, splicing images together and making them flow—phrasing them, in effect. And of course writing is related to music. And she thinks there is a parallel in the mathematical base of organization that is applied in music composition to running her own management company.

One task of Rocky Mountain Productions is to schedule Judy Collins' concerts. She usually plays 30 or more a year. She uses a guitar in concert less and less. At the beginning she found a guitar helpful, partly because she couldn't afford a band. But now she feels that the guitar separates her from the audience. She prefers to stand and sing, leaving musical accompaniment to the band. She also prefers audiences not larger than 3000 or 4000. Otherwise people can't hear or see her well enough. She hates the type of concert where the performer looks

like an ant on the stage.

Her main goal in how she sets up a concert is freedom of choice. She wants to be able to pick up a guitar and accompany herself if that feels right, or, more often, accompany herself on the piano. She wants to be able to take the audience wherever she wants. She tries to draw them in, to take them with her. That is part of the art of performing. She doesn't like to appear with another act as an opening, and rarely arranges to do so. She wants to sing for several hours, establish a mood. Her audiences are never raucous. They are generally quiet and intensely responsive.

During the time she was making *Antonia,* Judy was pretty withdrawn from music, and was, in fact, disgruntled about the music world in general. Many people thought she had retired, but it was not so. She was simply exploring another side of her talents. But after *Antonia* she wanted to make a new record.

She was unsure about which direction to go in, and spent a lot of time traveling around the world, looking for the right producer and engineer to work with. She realized that she didn't want to work in Los Angeles or London. She wanted to record in New York, so her private life would be less disturbed. Her friend Paul Simon recom-

mended Phil Ramone as engineer, and she managed to get Arif Mardin as producer. It was a perfect combination.

In 1975 they released her next album, *Judith,* a brilliant new album that rapidly went gold. In 1976 the same trio created Judy's most recent album, *Bread and Roses,* an exploratory and interesting effort.

Where will the multi-talented Judy Collins go next? Clearly she is not interested in fads or fashions. She follows her development as an artist with absolute integrity. She has no interest in success formulas, and that is, perhaps, one of the secrets of her long success.

She is thinking now of a Vegas show, or a one-woman Broadway show. She feels she is moving toward that because her concerts are becoming more theatrical, with elements of lighting and design increasingly important. She is still interested in acting, but is not interested in producing more films. "I don't think I *could* do that again." (Susan Elliott, *High Fidelity,* April 1977.)

She has never relinquished her early dream of becoming a concert pianist. She tries to practice every day and takes lessons, in the hopes of someday giving a classical concert. She is also interested in music for children. She has done several Sesame Street shows, and would like to develop an

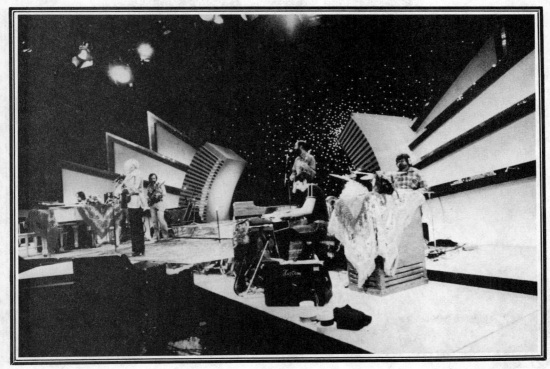

Andrew Kent/Mirage

Nancy Dubin

38

idea she has for an animated television special. She is fascinated by children and by the way they think.

Who is Judy Collins? She is certainly an intensely private person for one who is such a public figure. We know that she can be an actress, a writer, a songwriter, a film-maker, a feminist, and a mother. Most of all we know that she is a singer. In order to understand this rare person who combines elusiveness with straightforwardness, we must turn to the records, we must look to her music.

Andrew Kent/Mirage

Her Music

4.

Judy Collins' music has a remarkable range. Her earliest music was traditional folk, and then her voice was an alto. Her most recent record, *Bread and Roses,* is an eclectic collection of songs no longer recognizable as folk, and her voice has become a lovely soprano. There is a chameleon quality to Judy's talent; she is hard to describe, harder to define. Yet there is a subtle consistency to what she has accomplished musically.

Her earliest album, *A Maid of Constant Sorrow,* is interesting to go back and listen to, from the perspective of her later career. It is fairly clear in this album that she has not had formal training for either guitar or voice. There is a roughness, a simplicity to her approach that is moving, and that was in fact very fashionable in 1961, when the record was first released.

Judy was only 21 when this album was recorded, yet it has a quality of maturity, in terms of her interpretative powers, that belies her youth. Her diction has absolute clarity, her voice is richly expressive, and her sense of the dramatic nature of her material, the *story* of each song, is rendered in impeccably good taste.

The title song, "Maid of Constant Sorrow," gives us Judy's first public image:

> I am a maid of constant sorrow
> I've seen trials all of my days
> I'm going back to California
> Place where I was partly raised....

She presents us with a sad, lonesome song, an image of desolation.

This song is quickly followed by the robust "The Prickilie Bush," replacing the image of loneliness with one of betrayal and rescue. "The Prickilie Bush" tells the story of a man whose parents betray him but who is saved from hanging by his faithful lover paying a ransom.

Judy begins the next cut, "Wild Mountain Thyme," a capella, then is joined by the quietly supportive banjo accompaniment of Erik Darling. "Wild Mountain Thyme" is a Scottish song, lyrical in its tenderness. Collins' voice is strained and rough in the upper reaches on this song, revealing her lack of training.

"Tim Evans," the only "written" song on the album, is by the famed Ewan MacColl, and is an early protest song commemorating the unjust hanging of a man accused of murdering his wife and child.

Although almost all the songs on *A Maid of Constant Sorrow* are traditional, there is a consistency of theme, a concern with injustice toward men, especially in terms of war, and the mourning and sorrows of the women left at home:

> Oh woe be to the orders that marched
>   my love away
> And woe be to the bitter tears I shed
>   upon this day
> And woe be to the bloody wars of
>   High Germany
> For they've carried off my own
>   true love
> And left a broken heart to me

41

These lyrics from "Wars of Germany," which opens the second side of the album, presage the contemporary folk music that was starting to emerge, songs like Dylan's "Masters of War." But at this point singers like Collins were still making their views known through traditional songs.

"I Know Where I'm Going" is a defiant love song that spoke well to a generation most accurately characterized by its resistance to authority, especially parental authority, with its pressures to make conservative choices:

> I know where I'm going
> I know who's going with me
> I know who I love
> And the devil knows who I'll marry....

In the same vein, the song "John Riley," which Joan Baez also recorded, was a symbolic promise of faithfulness to men who were forced to either become exiles or else get drafted.

Judy Collins has said about this earliest album, "As I listen to the songs on the album, there is an almost painful quality of nostalgia to it all. It makes me almost physically unhappy, almost as if music were the only way I could get those feelings out; the longings and dreams I had in those days. I hear something lost, but hopeful." ("Going Home Again," Judy Collins; *Ms.* magazine, April 1973.)

Folk music attempts to capture the human experience in its most dramatic and moving and powerful moments: it is a distillation of drama. The art of the folksinger is to render specific something that is relatively general, fixed by tradition. In order to be effective, the folksinger must recreate the spark that initially triggered the song. That is part of the reason a folksinger seems to be more than a singer, a storyteller of sorts. And it is in this ability to recreate a song, to

David Gahr

make it new, that Judy Collins' great talent lies. Her diction, increasing the listener's opportunity to hear the words, is crucial to her work in a way that diction is not, for instance, important to the work of Joan Baez. What we cannot decipher in Baez's singing is compensated for by the ethereal beauty of her voice. Collins' voice, by comparison, is a lush, rich and much more vibrant instrument.

Listening to the second album, *Golden Apples of the Sun,* one is struck by a rapid vocal development. Where Collins' voice had been a husky alto in *A Maid of Constant Sorrow,* recorded eight months earlier, it is now becoming airier, purer. The phrasing is more confident and supple, forceful yet relaxed. Accompaniment is simple, as it was in the first album: a second guitar and a bass, instead of a second guitar and a banjo. And again, the music is predominantly traditional, public-domain music, with a special inclination to Scottish and Irish ballads.

The title song of *Golden Apples of the Sun* is a stunning rendition of a W.B. Yeats poem set to music. It tends to be more of an art song than a folk song. It has the ritualistic, repetitive quality of an incantation. The melody is haunting. Judy learned the song from another singer, Will Holt, at

the Gate of Horn. He made her a tape of it, but it took her more than a year to assimilate "Golden Apples of the Sun" and make it her own.

"Bonnie Ship the Diamond," the second cut on the record, is a robust, rollicking, celebratory song, different from the plaintive, bitter tunes that mostly characterize these early albums. It deals with the opening of the so-called Southerwest fisheries to whalermen, and conveys the happiness the sailors feel returning to port with money in hand, to celebrate with women.

The third cut is also a departure for Judy, a children's song, "Little Brown Dog." Collins says on the jacket notes that the song originally had had political implications, but that their meaning had been lost over the years.

The fourth cut is her first recorded black gospel song, "Twelve Gates to the City," a song she had heard the Rev. Gary Davis sing. The religious theme is contained in the following song, "Christ Child Lullaby." This was initially sung in Gaelic and was translated by Seamus Ennie, an Irish folklorist. Judy was drawn to the song because it is told from the unusual point of view of Jesus' mother, Mary.

The last cut on the first side is another song that Joan Baez also recorded, "Great

Jim Marshall

43

Selchie of Shule Skerry." This eerily beautiful ballad had its origin in the folklore of the supernatural in the Orkney Islands of Great Britain. The selchie is a being who is a seal in the ocean and an ordinary man when he comes ashore. The song tells of the selchie impregnating a woman, then returning to claim his son in exchange for a purse of gold. The selchie then foretells how the woman will marry a man who will kill both him and his son:

> And it shall come to pass on a summer's
>   day
> When the sun shines hot on every stone
> That I shall take my little wee son
> And I'll teach him how to swim the
>   foam.
>
> And you will marry a gunner good
> And a proud good gunner I'm sure he'll
>   be
> And he'll go out on a May morning
> And he'll kill both my wee son and me.
>
> And lo she did marry a gunner good
> And a proud good gunner I'm sure it
>   was he
> And the very first shot that e'er he did
>   shoot
> He killed the son and the great selchie.

This song gets its great power from making the conception of a child (and loss of one) a supernatural event, thereby tapping into the fundamental mystery of birth. According to Albert B. Friedman in the jacket notes, many families in the Scottish islands trace their ancestry to sealmen, and it is still a taboo for them to eat seal meat.

The second side of *Golden Apples of the Sun* opens with a Polish art song which second guitarist Walter Raim had translated and then arranged himself. "Tell Me Who I'll Marry" is sophisticated in construction, obviously composed rather than traditional, and provides Collins with an opportunity to show what a finely skilled singer she is becoming.

"Fannerio" is the first Collins song to hint of feminist concerns. It is one of a whole group of folksongs that tells of the casual relationships between soldiers and the women they encounter. In the spritely "Fannerio," a soldier is rewarded for his faithlessness by losing his life.

The third song, "Crow on the Cradle," is one of the two composed songs of the album. This composition by Sydney Carter is a bitter lullaby about the impossibility of raising children in a war-crazy world. The song portrays contemporary children as cursed by the spectre of war.

"Lark in the Morning" and "Sing Hallelujah" are both infectious, robust songs. "Shule Aroon," the last cut, is an Irish lament. Originally a Gaelic ballad of the 17th century, the song has survived in countless versions, one of which is "Johnny Has Gone for a Soldier."

In *Golden Apples of the Sun*, then, one can feel Judy Collins' growth as a singer, a maturation of range. However, there is a quality of chafing against the limitations of traditional material. In her third album, *Judy Collins #3*, she breaks away from traditional material almost completely. Her notes on the album jacket reflect her feelings for her own musical roots. She seems to realize that the material she has been recording, the traditional public-domain folk songs, are rather like studying textbooks. She recognizes that extraordinary, original folk material is emerging all around her, and sees that it does not come from a country tradition but from an urban one. What matters to her is to interpret the songs of the great contemporary writers—Bob Dylan and Bob Gibson and Woody Guthrie and Pete Seeger and Mike Settle and Fred Hellerman and Shel Silverstein and Jim Friedman. The album contains only one traditional song, "Bullgine Run," and she feels compelled to explain that she included it "just because I like it so much."

This departure into contemporary material proved an important one. She was learning to trust her own taste. She was also one of the first singers to interpret the brilliant songs of Bob Dylan, who became the spokesman for the conscience and sensibility of his generation in a way unparalleled in modern music. She has included two Dylan songs on the album, the wonderfully written "Masters of War" and the less chilling, entirely different, "Farewell."

"Farewell" seems a forerunner to later Dylan classics like "Don't Think Twice, It's All Right," and "It Ain't Me, Babe." Though it has rather conventional lyrics, one suspects Collins included it because it is so unlike Dylan's typically bitter work:

> So fare thee well my own true love
> We'll meet another day another time
> It's not the leaving that's grieving me
> But my true love who's bound to stay
>   behind . . . .

"Masters of War," on the other hand, is classical early Dylan, containing the almost unbearable bitterness and rage of the early Sixties, as Dylan began to give a voice to his generation. "Masters of War" is a stinging indictment of those who hide in their mansions while young people die, the generals behind their desks, safe from the front lines. "Even Jesus would never forgive what you do."

Collins cannot bring the rage to her voice that Dylan could, but on the other hand the purity of her voice, the clarity of her interpretation, reveal the beauty of the song, the purity of its conception, in a way Dylan's own version could not.

The themes of war and protest are fairly consistent in this album. "Anathea," the first cut on the album, is an eerily beautiful song generally credited to Lydia Wood. "Anathea" tells the story of a woman who tries to trade her virginity to save her imprisoned brother. Her brother tells her this won't work, the judge will simply use her and will still hang him:

> Anathea did not heed him
> Straight way to the judge went running
> In his golden bed at midnight
> There she heard the gallows groaning

> Anathea, Anathea, don't go into the
>   forest
> There among the green pines standing
> You will find your brother hanging.

A similar song in many ways is "In the Hills of Shiloh," by Shel Silverstein and Jim Friedman. "In the Hills of Shiloh" is about post-Civil War times, the Civil War being a means for examining the terrible destructions of war. "In the Hills of Shiloh" tells the story of Amanda, who wanders the hills of Shiloh in a yellowed wedding dress, waiting for her man to return, not able to understand that the war has been over forty years. This is basically a Faulknerian conception, an old woman whose mind is destroyed by war.

"Hey Nelly Nelly" is also by Shel Silverstein and Jim Friedman, but could not be more different from "In the Hills of Shiloh." The only similarity is that once again the Civil War era is the focus. Here we get a positive view of that war, its importance for the rights of black people. Abraham Lincoln is a character in this song, as are all those who fought for the freedom of the slaves. Unlike "In the Hills of Shiloh," "Hey Nelly Nelly" ends with a verse that brings it into the Sixties, and we understand that this

David Gahr

45

is really a song commemorating the hundred-year *anniversary* of the Civil War.

Another song of special significance on the album is "Deportee/Plane Wreck at Los Gatos," with lyrics by Woody Guthrie and melody by Marty Hoffman. This song is straight folk/protest music at its best. The song memorializes a group of Mexican laborers who, once the orchard crops were picked, were being deported to Mexico. Guthrie understands deeply the exploitation of poor laborers, useful as long as there are crops to pick at insulting wages, "aliens" after the crops are in. The cost of deporting them takes all the money most of them have earned, and by the time of their departure they have been pretty much dehumanized:

> **You won't have a name when you ride**
> **the big airplane**
> **For all they will call you will be**
> **deportees.**

When the plane crashes over Los Gatos, California, the laborers are killed, but the radio announces that they were only deportees.

The song "Bells of Rhymney" has lyrics by Idris Davies, and a melody by Pete Seeger. Judy performs it with a 12-string guitar backup, giving it a rich musical background. A more remarkable Seeger song is "Turn! Turn! Turn!," a musical setting of a passage from Ecclesiastes. This extraordinary conception leads to a lovely benedictive song, very peaceful and accepting, and quite different from most of the folk music of the early Sixties.

"Settle Down" is another wanderer's song. "Come Away, Melinda" is a rather melodramatic, sentimentalized song about the destructiveness of war. "The Dove," by Ewan MacColl, is a much better song about the evils of war, and Collins sings it a capella, as if to emphasize its purity.

Judy Collins #3 brought Collins fame. As a folk/protest singer she had hit full stride. Her fourth album was, appropriately, a live recording of her historic concert at Town Hall in New York City on March 21, 1964.

All songs except one on *The Judy Collins Concert* are new ones. She continues, as in *Judy Collins #3,* to record primarily folk/protest music by contemporary writers. She does one song by Bob Dylan, "The Lonesome Death of Hattie Carroll," a bitter Dylan ballad about the murder of a middle-aged black maid by a rich white man at a "Baltimore hotel society gathering."

Judy's talents as a storyteller are very prominent in this album, as are her leanings toward a country and western sound. "Me and My Uncle," by John Phillips, is a comic ballad about gambling, cowboys, murder, and betrayal. It parodies the usual notions of cowboy codes of honor.

She does one song by Fred Neil, the rousing "Tear Down the Walls":

> **The music's everywhere**
> **When every man is free . . . .**

Other western-influenced songs on the album are the traditional "Wild Rippling Water," and the songs of Billy Edd Wheeler and Tom Paxton. Judy does three songs by each of them.

David Gahr

Wheeler is a very talented writer with remarkable range. His beautiful "Winter Sky" is a deeply moving song, slow and strange. "And I feel like something's being born . . ." he says, trying to explore the feelings he gets looking at a winter sky. Wheeler grew up in a coal-mining town amid terrible poverty, and his two other songs on this album, done beautifully by Collins, are "Red-Winged Blackbird," and "Coal Tattoo," both about coal mining. Wheeler uses the red-winged blackbird as a symbol, combining the red of blood and death with the black of coal. It is a bitter, slow, careful song, well suited to Collins' precise diction. His "Coal Tattoo" is a fast-paced song, its rollicking quality in sharp contrast to the bitter words about a man trying to escape from a fate of working with coal.

The three songs by Paxton are also beautifully done. "Rambling Boy" and "Bottle of Wine" are both "up" songs about the wanderer's honorable life in America. Collins gets the audience to sing along with the chorus of both songs. Paxton's "The Last Thing on My Mind" is a very different kind of song, a love song about a man whose woman leaves him:

> Well I could have loved you better
> Didn't mean to be unkind
> You know that was the last thing on my mind.

The Judy Collins Concert also contains the eerie traditional song "Bonnie Boy is Young," which was also recorded, in

delay in the front rank of American balladeers."

The next two Judy Collins albums were transitional ones. The *Fifth Album* shows her loosening up a little, perhaps gaining confidence because of her growing popularity. She reaches out a little more too in terms of accompaniment, with a very effective mouth harp played by John Sebastian in Eric Anderson's song "Thirsty Boots," one of those wanderers songs that Collins favored so much in her early years. And Richard Farina, her dear and trusted friend, plays dulcimer on several songs, including his

Wide World Photos

slightly different form, by Joan Baez. It tells the story of a woman married to a teenage boy, her love for him, his brief life and untimely death.

The album is marred by the inclusion of the extremely sentimental "Medgar Evers Lullaby." This song by Richard Weissman pretends to be a lullaby for Medgar Evers' son, about why his father was killed. The racial murder of Medgar Evers was a cruel and shameful event in America's history, and does not need cheapening by this kind of treacly writing.

The building applause on the album reveals how receptive Collins' audience was that night, though. Robert Sherman of the *New York Times* wrote that "Judy Collins made her New York concert debut Saturday at Town Hall and established herself without

own "Pack Up Your Sorrows." One can feel Farina's influence on this album in several ways. The entire back cover is a long poem he wrote about Collins, and the depth of their friendship is publicly explored there.

Collins in these early albums sang so often about wanderers, loneliness, and disappointment (as well as her political concerns), one can almost feel her unhappiness in these years, the separation from her son still impossible to adjust to. Farina seemed to help her feel better. The refrain of his song, "pack up your sorrows, and give them all to me," has some meaning here. And maybe his good taste helped her too, since there are none of the sentimentalized, preachy songs like "Medgar Evers Lullaby" on this album.

The three Dylan songs she sings,

though, are among his loveliest and most accessible. Two are devastatingly lonely. "Tomorrow Is a Long Time" explores a feeling Collins must have often shared: "If tomorrow wasn't such a long time, then lonesome would mean nothing to me at all." And of course "Mr. Tambourine Man" is one of Dylan's most famous explorations of "there ain't no place I'm going to." The third Dylan tune, "Daddy You've Been on My Mind" was not as big a hit as "Tambourine Man," but in many ways it is one of Dylan's finest songs. It's an up-tempo, almost breezy sort of live-and-let-live love song, in which the singer makes it clear to her unseen lover that there are no demands, no strings—only the fact that he's been on her mind. Except this is repeated so often that by the end we're aware that she just may be protesting too much. There's a wonderful spirit to this song, this declaration of love and independence, without the anger or bitterness or sadness found in Dylan's other pieces of a similar nature.

There are politically conscious songs on this album, as there were on all the other ones. Phil Ochs' "In the Heat of the Summer" is an unsentimentalized examination of the race riots of the Sixties, as the frustration of blacks in the ghettos finally overran its bounds. "It Isn't Nice," by Malvina Reynolds and Barbara Dane, is a rousing protest song about social justice, about why so many young people were choosing to demonstrate, to go to jail, even though "it wasn't nice." However, this cut is really a leftover from the Town Hall concert, and in general the *Fifth Album* has a mellower sound than the earlier albums and seems more concerned with music than with political content.

In Judy's sixth album, *In My Life,* we witness a major change. All the pieces are arranged and conducted by Joshua Rifkin, who arranged much of the music for Nonesuch, Elektra's classical label. Judy sings with an orchestra, with delicate but full arrangements, and the difference in her sound is amazing. Her early classical roots are evident here in a faint but definite way, and these roots combine well with her still-growing interpretive powers.

In My Life was Judy Collins' first album to go gold. It's instructive to note that the only political song on the album is "La Colombe," by Jacques Brel, and one senses that Collins is singing it simply because she loves it.

There are several other major departures in *In My Life.* One is the presence of Broadway show music, an unheard-of choice for a folksinger, and as shocking in its way as the orchestral sounds are. And the show music sounds unmistakably *like* show music. "Pirate Jenny" by Brecht, Kurt Weill, and Marc Blitzstein deals with a woman's dreams of revenge. "Marat/Sade" is an even more startling choice for Judy, a medley of "Homage to Marat," "Marat We're Poor," "People's Reaction," and "Poor Old Marat." What these songs signify is Judy's growing independence. She is clearly letting the world know that she will go her own way.

Judy continues to pay tribute to Farina by recording his song "Hard Lovin' Loser," and she introduces a wonderful new songwriter, Randy Newman. Now, in the Seventies, Newman is well respected for his fine writing and the integrity and sophistication of his music, but when *In My Life* came out, Newman was almost unknown. Judy showed an integrity and good taste of her own by choosing Newman's "I Think It's Going to Rain Today" and by introducing Jacques Brel. However, her most amazing discovery for *In My Life* was the songwriter Leonard Cohen.

Cohen is a brilliant poet-songwriter, and Judy's version of his song "Suzanne" has become a classic of contemporary music. This haunting song's great power is hard to analyze, but people are tremendously moved by it. Judy also includes Cohen's "Dress Rehearsal Rag," a song as deeply about despair as is Dylan's "Tom Thumb's Blues," with which she opens the album. But Judy sings these despairing songs with a careful loveliness, and one senses that she is, despite her personal pain, beginning to transcend it through the sheer beauty of her music.

In the final cut on the album, the title song, Judy records a Beatles piece, a love song that she does very simply.

She trusted her own taste completely in *In My Life,* and not only brought several important new songwriters to the public eye but also produced her first gold record.

A year later she followed it with another gold record, *Wildflowers.* This album has a unity that none of Collins' previous records achieved. Once again she relies on Joshua Rifkin to arrange and conduct, and he sets up a heavily stringed, orchestrated sound, sweet and light and airy, for the songs Judy chooses. There are no political songs on the album. If there is a central theme, it is love. *Wildflowers* marries Judy's folk music past to a much more complex and individualistic art. If there are no theatrical songs on this album, she does continue to explore the work of Leonard Cohen, singing three of his songs: "Sisters of Mercy," "Priests," and "Hey, That's No Way to Say Goodbye." The first two of these are examples of the way Cohen tries to weave a religious sense into his fine poetry about love and loneliness and despair. In "Sisters of Mercy" Cohen observes:

> **When you're not feeling holy**
> **Your loneliness says that you've**
> **sinned,**

tapping into the confusion of loneliness and guilt so common to young people.

"Hey, That's No Way to Say Goodbye" is a fine and straightforward romantic love song, beautiful in its images, lyrical in its tenderness.

Judy started recording the songs of yet another relatively new songwriter on this album, the now-famous Joni Mitchell.

Mitchell's own voice is often too light, too sugary for her material, but Collins' rich, vibrant instrument gives Mitchell the showcase she deserves. "Both Sides Now" became one of Judy's biggest hits. She also sings another major Mitchell song, "Michael from Mountains."

The density, complexity, and beauty of Mitchell's lyrics and the equally haunting poetry of Leonard Cohen influenced the work of the other major new writer Judy Collins introduced on *Wildflowers:* herself. The album contains her first three recorded songs. "Since You Asked," the first song she ever wrote, is full of heavily worked nature imagery, "filling up the world with time, turning time to flowers." It is an impressive debut.

The other two original songs on the album, "Sky Fell," and "Albatross" are even better. "Albatross" is an incredibly dense, lovely poem, and even after much

study remains enigmatic, as much of Leonard Cohen's work does. "Sky Fell" is a love song, describing her despair when her lover leaves:

> The rain is falling
> Down along with the sky.

The rain becomes a symbol of grief, and the old image of the sky falling is made new.

Beauty is the word most often brought to mind in listening to *Wildflowers.* Judy could not have come farther from *A Maid of Constant Sorrow.* But if *Wildflowers* was an almost perfect exploration of a kind of soprano sweetness, a lyrical, stringed sound, Judy's next album, *Who Knows Where the Time Goes,* was another radical departure.

Many people, this author included, think that *Who Knows Where the Time Goes* is the finest album that Judy Collins has ever produced. This was the first and only album in which Judy allowed herself to be influenced by a contemporary rock sound, and the marriage of her soprano sweetness to electric guitar, electric piano, electric bass, and pedal steel guitar is a brilliant one. Stephen Stills of Crosby, Stills, Nash, & Young plays on almost every cut, and his influence is unmistakable. *Who Knows Where the Time Goes* was Collins' third gold record in a row.

Once again Judy relies on Dylan and Leonard Cohen, choosing one song by Dylan and two by Cohen, and including one of her own as well. However, the other songwriters on the album are new ones for her. Ian Tyson is one, whose remarkable "Someday Soon," with its country and western overtones, became one of Judy's biggest hit singles. Musically it is a simple, catchy song, and the lyrics present a touching story in which a young girl tells about her rodeo-obsessed boyfriend:

> He loves his damned old rodeo
> As much as he loves me

It is a perfect song to draw on Judy's immense storytelling powers, because the quick, bold-stroked portraits in the song— the girl, the boy, and the girl's parents— are so well drawn.

Even in a song like "Who Knows Where the Time Goes" written by Sandy Denny, where the sweet richness of Judy's voice and the precision of her diction are similar to some of her earlier songs, Stephen Stills on electric guitar and Chris Ethridge on electric bass build this slow-paced, laid-back

Len Steckler, Courtesy of Elektra Records

50

work to a passionate pitch.

The high quality of the accompaniment on this record would make it a classic. However, Judy's choice of material is equally superb. The album sounds so right, so *happy,* that even a bitter Dylan piece like "Poor Immigrant" becomes transformed into something beautiful. However, the last two cuts on the album, are, despite the amazing "Someday Soon" on Side One, among the best work Judy has ever done. "Bird on a Wire" by Leonard Cohen is unforgettable. True, this is one of Cohen's best songs, but Judy's performance of it is a tour de force. Singing with a strength unmatched in her other work (in this song and in the next one), Judy brings a passion to Cohen's mournful work that makes it work on a great number of levels. Even Adrienne Rich, a major American poet who has won the National Book Award as well as many others, quotes this song as an epigraph for one of her books, and the credit carefully reads that she is not just quoting Cohen's song, she is quoting it "as sung by Judy Collins."

Judy follows "Bird on a Wire" with her own arrangement/adaptation of the traditional song "Pretty Polly." It is hard to believe that she can surpass the preceding cut, but she does. "Pretty Polly" is done simply, slowly, but with an aura about it that is amazing. The song builds to a powerful, terrifying conclusion, taking full advantage of the force of her voice and the talented electric backup.

Perhaps because Judy had now produced three quite different gold records in a row, Elektra released a collection of her much earlier folk music, *Recollections.* This collection had two purposes: to show Judy's range to even more advantage, and to capitalize on her growing fame. All of the songs are from Judy's first five albums, her distinctly "folk" phase, and all are songs that are often requested when she sings in concert. There are three Dylan cuts, the moving "Daddy You've Been on My Mind," the beautiful love song "Tomorrow Is a Long Time," and the less effective "Farewell." Richard Farina's "Pack Up Your Sorrows" is included, but the rest of the collection seems fairly random: Gordon Lightfoot's "Early Morning Rain," Wheeler's "Winter Sky," Paxton's "The Last Thing on My Mind," among the choices. There are no selections from the first two albums, *A Maid of Constant Sorrow* and *Golden Apples of the Sun.* One suspects that the reason is that Collins' voice is so much less developed in these early records. Also, none of the selected songs, despite coming from the folk

Jim Marshall

51

era, are political. On the back of the album jacket is a picture of Judy with her son Clark, who had by then been returned to her. Perhaps the title *Recollections* symbolized for her that she was no longer afraid to remember, since she had Clark back now.

Judy's next new record came in 1970, a year after *Recollections.* One cannot help but wish that she had continued to delve into the rock/country sound of *Who Knows*

David Gahr

David Gahr

Where the Time Goes, since her foray into that sound had been so successful. But Judy let it be known that she found that sound boring. For someone with a classical background it was not challenging enough, despite its commercial success.

She took a big chance with her next album, *Whales and Nightingales,* and the chance paid off. This new album also went gold. *Whales and Nightingales* is extraordinary, for in it Judy more fully explored her classical influences. There is some fairly daring material, even though she continued to draw on contemporary musicians for some of the cuts: Brel, Dylan, Seeger, Joan Baez, and herself.

Judy does Joan Baez's beautiful "Song for David" as her first cut. Baez wrote this song for her husband, David Harris, while she was pregnant and he was going off to prison for draft resistance. Though overwritten, the song is moving partly because it

was public knowledge that Harris was going to prison for his political beliefs. In the song Baez reasures him:

> The stars in your sky are the stars in
>   mine
> And both prisoners of this life are
>   we. . . .

It is interesting for Judy to sing Joan Baez's song, and a sign of Judy's integrity. Collins is often compared to Baez, and the comparison is unfair and glib, since Baez relies almost entirely on the ethereal beauty of her voice, and Collins is more adventurous, more eclectic and inventive. For Collins to

John Grissim

53

want to interpret Baez's writing is both a tribute and a way of emphasizing their differences.

"Farewell to Tarwathie" is one of the boldest strokes in her entire repertoire. Judy sings a whalermen's song, not to instrumental accompaniment but to the background sounds of humpback whales. The record those sounds are taken from, *Songs of the Humpback Whale,* is in itself amazing. For Judy to combine this whale-hunting song with the beautiful sounds of the whales themselves is a brilliant and ironic idea. The song is startling, original and lovely.

If *Who Knows Where the Time Goes* experimented with contemporary rock and drew heavily on Judy's interpretive story-telling powers, *Whales and Nightingales* is its opposite. One of the songs on this album is in French, as if Judy wanted to make clear that it was the *music,* the *sound* that mattered to her, not the "message." And two of the songs on this album are instrumentals, a mind-boggling move for a singer. "Gene's Song," by Gene Murrow, is simply a beautiful melody, and "Nightingale II" is an instrumental, free adaptation of Judy's wonderfully lyrical "Nightingale I." It is as if, on this album, Judy wished to emphasize her general musical talents rather than her singing abilities, and also wished to give freer play to her classical orientation. "Nightingale II" sounds suspiciously like classical music. And though she worked with rock musicians on *Who Knows Where the Time Goes,* in *Whales and Nightingales* she returns to Joshua Rifkin for collaboration.

Another remarkable song on this album is "Amazing Grace." For Judy to try a black spiritual may seem peculiar, but even more peculiar is that it works. The single of "Amazing Grace" was a hit, and perhaps the secret of its success for Judy was that she did not attempt a "black" sound, which many white musicians do when they sing black music. Singing a capella, she sounds like no one but herself.

Discounting the reprise record *Recollections,* Judy had now had four gold records in a row, with wildly different material and approaches.

Her next album was, puzzlingly, not a commercial success compared to the records that had preceded it. Maybe Judy's public was disappointed by *Living,* which had none of the boldness of *Who Knows*

Alanna Nash

Where the Time Goes or *Wildflowers* or *Whales and Nightingales.*

She fell back on her standard elements in this album, songs by Cohen and Dylan and Joni Mitchell, along with some songs of her own, and though the album is superb in parts, it also feels uneven. Cohen's two songs are brilliant. "Joan of Arc," the first cut on the album, is a powerful, unsettling tone poem reminiscent of "Suzanne" in

John Grissim

terms of making women mysterious, though "Suzanne" was somehow transcendent, and "Joan of Arc" comes across as sad, with Joan a kind of Christ-figure with fragile faith. Cohen's other song is "Blue Raincoat," which takes the form of a letter to a former rival and friend, and is a powerful piece of writing, Cohen managing to convey all the complexity of feeling that such a situation would entail.

The "Vietnam Love Song" by Arnold Black and Eric Bentley is, unfortunately, too blatantly political to have much depth, though the melody is sweet. Collins give Ian Tyson's "Four Strong Winds" a lovely rendition.

"Easy Times," the song Judy wrote with Stacy Keach for Keach's film "The Repeater" about prison recidivism, is one of the best songs on the record. It has the form of a love letter from a woman whose man is in prison. She asks, "Will there ever be a time tomorrow?"

The best song on the album is entirely by Judy Collins. It is "Song for Judith (Open the Door)," and a happier, more pleasing song is hard to think of for comparisons. The refrain of the song,

Herb Goro, courtesy of Elektra Records

Open the door and come on in
I'm so glad to see you, my friend
You're like a rainbow
Coming around the bend . . . .

is very powerful. The song gets a lot of mileage from its title, making clear that the song is not only about friendship but also about self-love. Judy sings of how she had lost herself in her unhappiness, now understands that everyone has hard times. The celebratory nature of the song, its general high quality, augered well for the future of Judy's songwriting.

The album is marred by a six-minute version of "Just Like Tom Thumb's Blues," by Bob Dylan, a song Judy had already done a powerful version of in her earlier album *In My Life*. One cannot help wondering if this live recording is a form of padding, and if it signals a confusion in Judy about which direction go to in. Despite the album's power, it leaves the careful listener with an uneasiness about Judy's future. Was it possible her talent had played itself out?

This fear was compounded by her next recording, *Colors of the Day: The Best of Judy Collins*. Often when a recording company puts out a "best of," it is because the artist has burned out, and they want to milk a last few sales from her fans. *Colors of the Day* contains some of Judy's most extraordinary songs, cuts like "Someday Soon" and "Suzanne" and "Farewell to Tarwathie." One can only wonder why Brel's "Sons of"

Joseph Stevens

David Gahr. Judy, Clive Davis and Marge Guthrie

and Donovan's "Sunny Goodge Street" are included here while songs like "Bird on a Wire" and "Song for Judith (Open the Door)" are not. However, possibly because so many Collins classics had not been included on one album before, possibly because people feared her career was over, *Colors of the Day* went gold.

Judy fooled the critics by producing, some eight months later, one of her most remarkable albums, if not her most successful commercially. *True Stories and Other Dreams* was the first Collins album to be comprised predominantly of her own material. Judy had taken the promise of her earlier songwriting to a new level.

As she did in *Living,* Judy has returned here to an electric sound, but the electric guitar is combined with a variety of instruments, depending on the cut—congas and bongos, autoharp, concertina, fiddle, banjo, and others. The sound is a new one, very different from the albums she worked on with Joshua Rifkin, but free of the country and western/rock sound of *Who Knows Where the Time Goes.* Judy was once again making her own direction.

The lead cut, "Cook with Honey," on *True Stories,* however, was not written by Judy but by Valerie Carter, a young California writer. Judy got the song from a cameraman friend, who knew Valerie. The song is warm, homey, nice to listen to, and gave Judy her first hit single in quite a while. Another remarkable song on the album was written by Bob Ruzicka, a Nashvile dentist who, among other things, had gone to Alaska for a year to give free dental treatment to the Eskimos. Ruzicka's song is called "The Dealer (Down and Losin')." A card game becomes a metaphor for many things about life. Judy sings, "You can't win and you can't break even, you can't get out of the game . . . ." Nevertheless, it's a "foolish man who tries to bluff the dealer."

There is more political music on this album than Judy has shown interest in for a long time. She does a powerful version of Tom Paxton's song about the Attica prison rebellion called "The Hostage." The song is written from the point of view of a guard who is taken hostage by the prisoners. The guard quickly figures out that if the prisoners were going to kill him, they would have done so immediately, so he relaxes, waiting to be freed. Then the police drop tear gas and storm the prison, shooting anything that moves. The hostage and his friends are all

59

shot by the police. He takes a second bullet while he's on the ground. The experience is a radicalizing one, as he realizes the "governor cut my throat and cut it good," that his life meant as little to the powers-that-be as the prisoners' lives did.

Even more remarkable is Judy's own political song, "Che," about the death of the South American revolutionary Che Guevara. It is one of Judy's most ambitious efforts, a 7½-minute cut, musically complex and beautifully written. The song has a message that becomes its refrain:

Continue with your work
Continue with your talk
You have it in your hands
To own your lives

The strength of *True Stories* is Judy's original songs. Besides "Che," there are two songs about her family, "Secret Gardens" and "Holly Ann." "Secret Gardens" is a song she described composing in her *Ms.* magazine article in 1973. "Holly Ann" is about Judy's younger sister, a weaver who lives north of San Francisco with a man who built his own house. The song, a loving, careful, unpretentious portrait of Holly Ann, says "it's peaceful where she's living."

Judy also does a lively original song called "Fishermen Song," which is about fishermen, of course, but works also in a broad allegorical way. Judy seems to be saying we can learn from the fishermen, who have acquired patience in their lives, who don't catch more than they can sell in a day, and who know the "day's for work and night's the time to go dancing."

But Judy's best song on *True Stories* is "Song for Martin," a moving tribute to a friend who committed suicide. Collins tries to understand her friend's loneliness, "the heart that sorrow broke in you." She tells us about Martin, who lived in Arizona, and whom she wished she had not lost touch with so that at the end of his life their relationship consisted of talking on the phone once or twice a year. She deals simply with the inevitable guilt that a friend's suicide causes: "I know I let you down somewhere."

Whether it was because *True Stories* was not a success commercially, whether it was just because she was working so hard on her movie about Antonia Brico, whether she had simply gotten tired of music, Judy did not release another album for more than two years. Ever since her recording career began in 1961, there had not been such a gap in her work.

When, in 1975, she produced her fourteenth album, *Judith,* she made it another artistic departure. *Judith* sounds like no previous Collins record.

The difference seems to lie basically

Alvan Meyerowitz

Joseph Stevens

Nancy Dubin

with Judy's new producer, Arif Mardin. Mardin creates a "professional" feel in Judy's music that is perhaps overpolished, overworked. Those who value primarily Judy's *artistry,* her originality, may be put off by this new slickness. However, the album was certainly a commercial success: it rapidly went gold.

The most impressive song on *Judith* is Stephen Sondheim's "Send in the Clowns," from the Broadway production *A Little Night Music.* A difficult melody for most singers, Judy's version was better than even Sinatra's, went high on the single charts, and won her a Grammy.

Judy goes into the past for several cuts on this album. "Brother Can You Spare a Dime" is one of those bitter Depression songs, and "I'll Be Seeing You" is a lovely Thirties melody by Sammy Fain and Irving Kahal. From more contemporary sources, Judy does beautiful versions of "The Moon Is a Harsh Mistress" by Jimmy Webb and "Angel, Spread Your Wings" by Danny O'Keefe.

A less successful venture is her inclusion of a Stones song, "Salt of the Earth," by Mick Jagger and Keith Richard. In Judy's version her voice is subordinated to drums, bass, and electric piano, and by a group of background singers. Judy is simply not suited to a rock song, even though she tries hard to make it her own. The Stones version, like most of their music, has a bitter, ironic, almost vicious edge. Although the song is supposed to be a toast to the salt of the earth, the common people, the Stones' lyrics read:

> They don't look real to me
> In fact they look so strange . . . .

Judy changes this to:

> They look so real to me
> And they look so much in pain . . . .

Judy takes the edge off the song, makes the song a sweet anthem, and thereby a mockery of the Stones' more complex meaning.

The best songs on *Judith,* besides "Send in the Clowns," are ones that Collins wrote herself. Of these three—"Houses," "Song for Duke," and "Born to the Breed"— "Houses" is the least successful. The song just doesn't seem to come together, perhaps because of Mardin's overproduction. "Song for the Duke," on the other hand, Judy's tribute to Duke Ellington, is very effective. She sings:

> The man was a hero
> He played the music of our souls . . . .

Her best original song on *Judith* is "Born to the Breed," written for her son. In this song Judy acknowledges her son's need to explore himself even though that means leaving home to travel with a rock and roll band. She goes back through details of their lives together, and though she is frightened for him ("Does that old parka keep you dry?") understands that he is doing what he has to do:

> I know you're gonna make it
> You were born to the breed.

Andrew Kent/Mirage

In Judy Collins' most recent album, *Bread and Roses,* she is still working with Arif Mardin, but seems to have finally subordinated his lavish productions to the merits of her voice. Although this album has not gone gold, in many ways it is superior to *Judith.*

The dominant tone of *Bread and Roses* is an easy, swinging one, but the album is not happy or fun the way, for instance, *True Stories,* despite its political songs, was. There is an earnestness about *Bread and Roses* that is part of its power.

The title song is a poem by James

Previous page: Richard MacCaffree

Mary Ellen Mark, courtesy of Elektra Records

Oppenheim, a Midwesterner who moved to New York as a child and became one of the early Greenwich Village "bohemians." Oppenheim died in the early Thirties. Mimi Farina set the poem to music, turning it into a moving anthem about the liberation of women. Oppenheim understands that the liberation of women is necessary, a good thing, for men as well as women:

The rising of the women means the rising of the race . . . .

Judy told Ernest Leogrande of United Features (1976), "I love the song, which is

works of intensity which haven't been done to death by other singers. This latest album is not catchy or easy to listen to. It demands concentration, but the concentration certainly pays off.

In addition to the title song, there is another political piece: "Plegaria a un Labrador," the lyrics by Victor Jara. Victor Jara was a Chilean singer who, like thousands of others, was imprisoned in Santiago University stadium when the military junta overthrew Allende. Allende was perhaps the most famous victim of the junta's slaughters, but Victor Jara, in his martyrdom, gave

Nancy Dubin

always the first test for me of whether a song works. I love doing other people's work. My first career is as pianist and singer and only secondary as a writer." This is an amazingly selfless thing for such a fine songwriter to say. But perhaps Judy Collins' durability as a singer can partly be traced to the selflessness of her approach to music. She has certainly been responsible for discovering many important songwriters.

In her last two albums, Judy seems to have been poking around in the Thirties and Forties for new material, as well as searching, as usual, through contemporary songs. The titles on *Bread and Roses* are bold partly because they are so unfamiliar. Judy, as usual, has been searching for

voice to the everyday people, the laborers, who were also, if they were at all political, sacrificed. Jara's hands were broken before he was finally killed. His last poem was smuggled out of the stadium. It is a prayer to the working class:

**Take your brother's hand, so you can grow.
We'll go together, united by blood.
Now and in the hour of our death.
Amen.**

Judy sings Jara's poem, in both English and Spanish, with the political passion that was characteristic of her early work. It is nice to see Collins finding her political roots again, and finding them in a way that is not sim-

plistic, in this song and on *Bread and Roses.*

Almost all the other tunes on *Bread and Roses* are love songs. Exceptions are "Marjorie," a brief children's round for which Judy sings all the parts, and "King David," a bluesy tone poem written in the early Twenties by Herbert Howells and the poet Walter de la Mare. The song shows off Collins' superb voice in all its fine range and sensitivity.

One especially effective love song is Leonard Cohen's "Take This Longing," an almost pathetically needful poem pleading with a lover to

> Let me see your beauty broken down
> As you would do
> For one you love.

Cohen is talking about how we mystify our lovers, how real love does not require such mystification.

Many of the love songs are about loss. Judy's own "Out of Control" speaks with no direct negativity about being out of control in love, and the song has an up sound; but nevertheless there is an unsettling quality about it, an implication that falling in love is equivalent to losing your mind.

"Everything Must Change," a beautiful, catchy song that attempts to be accepting about loss, is one of the most successful tunes on the album, and was released as a single. But "Come Down in Time" by Elton John and Bernie Taupin is just too melancholy to interpret happily. "Love Hurts," by Andrew Gold, is one of the finest cuts on the album, but its message is evident.

There is a positive element in the love songs that open Side Two of the album, "Spanish is the Loving Tongue," a Thirties song that is extraordinarily lovely, and "I Didn't Know About You," a song by Duke Ellington and Bob Russell. Remembering Judy's tribute to the Duke on *Judith,* that she chooses to sing one of his most beautiful songs here is moving in itself.

Where will Judy Collins go in the future? Getting her start in the folk/protest movement of the early Sixties, she has long since outlived that phase and has continued to be courageously creative, sometimes brilliant, sometimes only searching. At this point in her life Judy Collins has accomplished many things, made 15 albums in 16 years, been consistently political in her life, protected her privacy as much as possible, hosted television shows, acted in a play, established a solid reputation as a songwriter, and produced and co-directed a brilliant movie. She has always conducted herself with profound integrity, and those of us who would like to predict her future course will just have to be patient and wait and see where she chooses to go next.

Nancy Dubin

Discography

Previous page: David Gahr

Nancy Dubin

5.

7E 1076	Bread and Roses (Gold)	*August 25, 1976* Producer: Arif Mardin
7E 1032	Judith (Gold)	*March 24, 1975* Producer: Arif Mardin
75053	True Stories & Other Dreams	*January 18, 1973* Producer: Mark Abramson & Judy Collins
75030	Colors of the Day (Gold)	*May 8, 1972* Producer: Mark Abramson
75014	Living	*November 2, 1971* Producer: Mark Abramson
75010	Whales & Nightingales (Gold)	*November 12, 1970* Producer: Mark Abramson
74055	Recollections	*July, 1969* Producer: Mark Abramson
74033	Who Knows Where the Time Goes (Gold)	*November, 1968* Producer: David Anderle
74012	Wildflowers (Gold)	*November, 1967* Producer: Mark Abramson
74027	In My Life (Gold)	*November, 1966* Producer: Mark Abramson
7300	Fifth Album	*November, 1965* Production Supervisor: Jac Holzman Recording Director: Mark Abramson
7280	JC Concert	*October, 1964* Producer: Jac Holzman & Mark Abramson
7242	Judy Collins #3	*March, 1964* Producer: Mark Abramson & Jac Holzman
7222	Golden Apples of the Sun	*June, 1962* Production Supervisor: Jac Holzman
7209	A Maid of Constant Sorrow	*October, 1961* *Production Supervisor: Jac Holzman*

All songs traditional unless otherwise noted

Maid of Constant Sorrow
EKS 7209, released 10/61

Maid of Constant Sorrow
The Pricklie Bush
Wild Mountain Thyme
Tim Evans—*E. MacColl*
Sailor's Life
Bold Fenian Men
Wars of Germany
O Daddy Be Gay
I Know Where I'm Going
John Riley
Pretty Saro
The Rising of the Moon

Golden Apples of the Sun
EKS 7222, released 7/62

Golden Apples of the Sun—*W.B. Yeats, Judy Collins*
Bonnie Ship the Diamond
Little Brown Dog
Twelve Gates to the City
Christ Child Lullaby
Great Selchie of Shule Skerry (Child #113)
Tell Me Who I'll Marry
Fannerio
Crow on the Cradle—*S. Carter*
Lark in the Morning
Sing Hallelujah—*M. Settle*
Shule Aroon

No. 3
EKS 7243, released 3/64

Anathea
Bullgine Run
Farewell—*B. Dylan*
Hey Nelly Nelly—*Silverstein, Friedman*
Ten O'Clock All Is Well—*Camp, Gibson*
The Dove—*E. MacColl*
Masters of War—*B. Dylan*
In the Hills of Shiloh—*Silverstein, Friedman*
The Bells of Rhymney—*Davies, Seeger*
Deportee—*W. Guthrie, Hoffman*
Settle Down—*Settle*
Come Away Melinda—*Minkoff, Hellerman*
Turn! Turn! Turn!/To Everything There Is a Season—*Ecclesiastes, Seeger*

Concert/Live
EKS 7280, released 10/64

Winter Sky—*B. Wheeler*
That Was the Last Thing on My Mind—*T. Paxton*
Tear Down the Walls—*F. Nell*
Bonnie Boy Is Young—*arranged by J. Collins*
Me and My Uncle—*J. Phillips*
The Lonesome Death of Hattie Carroll—*B. Dylan*
Wild Rippling Water—*Traditional, arranged by M. Robbins*
Cruel Mother—*arranged by J. Collins*
Ramblin' Boy—*T. Paxton*
Coal Tattoo—*B. Wheeler*

Jim Marshall

74

Bottle of Wine—*T. Paxton*
Red-Winged Blackbird—*J. Jaffe*
Medgar Evers Lullaby—*R. Weisman*
Hey Nelly Nelly—*S. Silverstein, J. Friedman*

Fifth Album
EKS 7300, released 11/65

Pack Up Your Sorrows—*R. Farina, P. Marden*
The Coming of the Roads—*B. Wheeler*
So Early, Early in the Spring—*arranged by J. Collins*
Tomorrow Is a Long Time—*B. Dylan*
Daddy, You've Been on My Mind—*B. Dylan*
Thirsty Boots—*E. Anderson*
Mr. Tambourine Man—*B. Dylan*
Lord Gregory—*arranged by J. Collins*
In the Heat of the Summer—*P. Ochs*
Early Morning Rain—*G. Lightfoot*
Carry It On—*G. Turner*
It Isn't Nice—*M. Reynolds, B. Dane*

In My Life
EKS 7320, released 11/66

Tom Thumb's Blues—*B. Dylan*
Hard Lovin' Loser—*R. Farina*
Pirate Jenny—*Brecht, Weil, Blitzstein*
Suzanne—*L. Cohen*
La Columbe—*Brel, Clayre*
Marat/Sade—*R. Peaslee*
    (Homage to Marat, Marat We're Poor, People's
    Reaction, Poor Old Marat)
I Think It's Going to Rain Today—*R. Newman*
Sunny Goodge Street—*Donovan*

Liverpool Lullaby—*S. Kelly*
Dress Rehearsal Rag—*L. Cohen*
In My Life—*Lennon, McCartney*

Wildflowers
EKS 74012, released 11/67

Michael from Mountains—*J. Mitchell*
Since You Asked—*J. Collins*
Sisters of Mercy—*L. Cohen*
Priests—*L. Cohen*
A Ballata of Frencesco Landini: Lasso! di donna
Both Sides Now—*J. Mitchell*
La Chanson des Vieux Amants—*Brel, Jouannest*
Sky Fell—*J. Collins*
Albatross—*J. Collins*
Hey, That's No Way to Say Goodbye—*L. Cohen*

Who Knows Where the Time Goes
EKS 74033, released 11/68

Hello, Hooray—*R. Kempf*
Story of Isaac—*L. Cohen*
My Father—*J. Collins*
Someday Soon—*I. Tyson*
Who Knows Where the Time Goes—*S. Denny*
Pity the Poor Immigrant—*B. Dylan*
First Boy I Lived—*R. Williamson*
Bird on the Wire—*L. Cohen*
Pretty Polly

Jim Marshall

Recollections
EKS 74055, released 7/69

Mr. Tambourine Man—*B. Dylan*
Winter Sky—*B. Wheeler*
Last Thing on My Mind—*T. Paxton*
Bells of Rhymney—*Davies, Seeger*
Farewell—*B. Dylan*
Pack up Your Sorrows—*R. Farina, P. Marden*
Tomorrow Is a Long Time—*B. Dylan*
Early Morning Rain—*G. Lightfoot*
Anathea
Turn! Turn! Turn!—*Ecclesiastes, Seeger*
Daddy, You've Been on My Mind—*B. Dylan*

Whales and Nightingales
EKS 75010, released 11/70

Song for David—*J. Baez*
Sons of—*Brel, Jouannest, Blau, Shuman*
The Patriot Game—*D. Behan*
Prothalamium—*M. Sahl, A. Kramer*
Oh, Had I a Golden Thread—*P. Seeger*
Gene's Song—*Arranged and adapted by
     G. Morrow*
Farewell to Tarwathie—*Arranged and adapted by
     J. Collins*
Time Passes Slowly—*B. Dylan*
Marieke—*Brel, Jouannest*
Nightingale I—*J. Collins*
Nightingale II—*J. Collins, J. Rifkin*
Simple Gifts
Amazing Grace

Living
EKS 75014, released 11/71

Song for Judith—*J. Collins*
All Things Are Quite Silent—*Arranged and
     adapted by J. Collins*
Joan of Arc—*L. Cohen*
Four Strong Winds—*I. Tyson*
Vietnam Love Song—*A. Black, E. Bently*
Innisfree—*W.B. Yeats, H. Camp*
Easy Times—*S. Keach, J. Collins*
Chelsea Morning—*J. Mitchell*
Blue Raincoat—*L. Cohen*
Just Like Tom Thumb's Blues—*B. Dylan*

Colors of the Day
EKS 75030, released 5/72

Someday Soon—*I. Tyson*
Since You Asked—*J. Collins*
Both Sides Now—*J. Mitchell*
Sons of—*Brel, Jouannest, Blau, Shuman*
Suzanne—*L. Cohen*
Farewell to Tarwathie
Who Knows Where the Time Goes—*S. Denny*
Sunny Goodge Street—*Donovan*
My Father—*J. Collins*
In My Life—*Lennon, McCartney*
Albatross—*J. Collins*
Amazing Grace

Howard Brainen

76

True Stories and Other Dreams
EKS 75053, released 1/73

Cook with Honey—*V. Carter*
So Begins the Task—*S. Stills*
Fisherman Song—*J. Collins*
The Dealer (Down & Losin')—*B. Ruzicka*
Secret Gardens—*J. Collins*
Holly Ann—*J. Collins*
the Hostage—*T. Paxton*
Song for Martin—*J. Collins*
Che—*J. Collins*

Judith
EKS 7E-1032, released 3/75

The Moon Is a Harsh Mistress—*J. Webb*
Angel Spread Your Wings—*D. O'Keefe*
Houses—*J. Collins*
The Lovin' of the Game—*P. Garvey*
Song for Duke—*J. Collins*
Send in the Clowns—*S. Sondheim*
Salt of the Earth—*M. Jagger, K. Richard*
Brother Can You Spare A Dime—*J. Gorney,*
    E.Y. Harburg
City of New Orleans—*S. Goodman*
I'll Be Seeing You—*S. Fair, I. Cahal*
Pirate Ships—*W. Waldman*
Born to the Breed—*J. Collins*

Bread and Roses
EKS 1076, released 8/76

Bread and Roses—*M. Farina, J. Oppenheim*
Everything Must Change—*B. Inghner*
Special Delivery—*B. Mernit*
Out of Control—*J. Collins*
Plegaria A Un Labrador—*V. Jara*
Come Down in Time—*E. John, B. Taupin*
Spanish Is a Loving Tongue—*C. Badger Clark Jr.,*
    M. Williams
I Didn't Know about You—*B. Russell,*
    Duke Ellington
Take This Longing—*L. Cohen*
Love Hurts—*A. Gold*
Marjorie—*Arranged by J. Collins*
King David—*W. De La Mare, H. Howells*

Richard MacCaffree

77